GO! with Microsoft®

Internet Explorer® 9

Getting Started

Shelley Gaskin and Robert L. Ferrett

AF869860

PEARSON

Boston Columbus Indianapolis New York San Francisco Upper Saddle River
Amsterdam Cape Town Dubai London Madrid Milan Munich Paris Montreal Toronto
Delhi Mexico City São Paulo Sydney Hong Kong Seoul Singapore Taipei Tokyo

Editor in Chief: Michael Payne
Executive Editor: Jenifer Niles
Product Development Manager: Laura Burgess
Editorial Assistant: Carly Prakapas
VP/Director of Business & Technology Marketing: Patrice Lumumba Jones
Marketing Coordinator: Susan Osterlitz
Marketing Assistant: Darshika Vyas
Associate Managing Editor: Camille Trentacoste
Senior Production Project Manager/IT Procurement Lead: Natacha Moore
Senior Operation Manager/Site Lead: Nick Sklitsis
Senior Art Director: Jonathan Boylan
Cover Photo: © Ben Durrant
Associate Director of Design: Blair Brown
Director of Media Development: Cathi Profitko
Senior Media Project Manager, Editorial: Alana Coles
Media Project Manager, Production: John Cassar
Full-Service Project Management: PreMediaGlobal
Composition: PreMediaGlobal
Printer/Binder: Quad/Graphics
Cover Printer: Lehigh-Phoenix Color/Hagerstown
Text Font: Bookman Light

Credits and acknowledgments borrowed from other sources and reproduced, with permission, in this textbook appear on the appropriate page within text.

Microsoft and/or its respective suppliers make no representations about the suitability of the information contained in the documents and related graphics published as part of the services for any purpose. All such documents and related graphics are provided "as is" without warranty of any kind. Microsoft and/or its respective suppliers hereby disclaim all warranties and conditions with regard to this information, including all warranties and conditions of merchantability, whether express, implied or statutory, fitness for a particular purpose, title and non-infringement. In no event shall microsoft and/or its respective suppliers be liable for any special, indirect or consequential damages or any damages whatsoever resulting from loss of use, data or profits, whether in an action of contract, negligence or other tortious action, arising out of or in connection with the use or performance of information available from the services.

The documents and related graphics contained herein could include technical inaccuracies or typographical errors. Changes are periodically added to the information herein. Microsoft and/or its respective suppliers may make improvements and/or changes in the product(s) and/or the program(s) described herein at any time.

Microsoft® and windows® are registered trademarks of the microsoft corporation in the U.S.A. And other countries. This book is not sponsored or endorsed by or affiliated with the microsoft corporation.

Copyright © 2013 by Pearson Education, Inc. as Prentice Hall. All rights reserved. Manufactured in the United States of America. This publication is protected by Copyright, and permission should be obtained from the publisher prior to any prohibited reproduction, storage in a retrieval system, or transmission in any form or by any means, electronic, mechanical, photocopying, recording, or likewise. To obtain permission(s) to use material from this work, please submit a written request to Pearson Education, Inc., Permissions Department, One Lake Street, Upper Saddle River, New Jersey 07458, or you may fax your request to 201-236-3290.

Many of the designations by manufacturers and sellers to distinguish their products are claimed as trademarks. Where those designations appear in this book, and the publisher was aware of a trademark claim, the designations have been printed in initial caps or all caps.

Library of Congress Cataloging-in-Publication Data

Gaskin, Shelley.
GO! with Internet explorer : getting started / Shelley Gaskin and Robert L. Ferrett.
p. cm.
Includes index.
ISBN 978-0-13-293454-1 (alk. paper)
1. Microsoft Internet explorer. 2. Internet. I. Ferrett, Robert. II. Title.
TK5105.883.M53G3925 2011
004.67'8—dc23

2011043991

10 9 8 7 6 5 4 3 2 1

PEARSON

ISBN-10: 0-13-293454-X
ISBN-13: 978-0-13-293454-1

Contents

GO! Walkthrough vi

Internet Explorer 9

Chapter 1 Exploring the World Wide Web with Internet Explorer 9 1

PROJECT 1A Browsing the Web with Internet Explorer 9 2

Objective 1 Use Tabbed Browsing 3
Activity 1.01 Using Tabbed Browsing 3
Activity 1.02 Using the Tab List, the Taskbar, and Shortcuts to Navigate Among Open Tabs 9
Activity 1.03 Using Tear-Off Tabs to View Tabs Side-By-Side and Create Shortcuts on the Taskbar 13

Objective 2 Organize Favorites 15
Activity 1.04 Organizing Favorites and Creating a Favorites Folder 16
Activity 1.05 Using the Favorites Bar 19

Objective 3 Manage Browsing History and Browse with InPrivate 20
Activity 1.06 Viewing and Deleting Browsing History 21
Activity 1.07 Using InPrivate Browsing 23

Objective 4 Print, Zoom, and Change the Text Size of Web Pages 24
Activity 1.08 Printing Web Pages 24
Activity 1.09 Zooming and Changing Web Page Text Size 27

Objective 5 Save Web Page Information 28
Activity 1.10 Saving Web Page Information 28

Objective 6 Manage Add-ons 31
Activity 1.11 Managing Add-ons 31

PROJECT 1B Searching with Search Tools and Using the Web Safely 34

Objective 7 Search the Internet 35
Activity 1.12 Searching the Internet 35

Objective 8 Subscribe to and View an RSS Feed 37
Activity 1.13 Subscribing to and Viewing an RSS Feed 38

Objective 9 Use Web Slices, Accelerators, and Suggested Sites 41
Activity 1.14 Using Web Slices 41
Activity 1.15 Using Accelerators 43

Objective 10 Block Pop-up Windows and Use the Notification Bar 46
Activity 1.16 Using the Internet Explorer 9 Pop-up Blocker and Notification Bar 46

Objective 11 Protect Against Malware 47
Activity 1.17 Protecting Against Malware 48

Objective 12 Protect Your Data **49**
Activity 1.18 Protecting Your Data 49
Summary, Key Terms, Matching, and Multiple Choice 52–53

Glossary **G-1**
Index **I-1**

About the Authors

Shelley Gaskin, Series Editor, is a professor in the Business and Computer Technology Division at Pasadena City College in Pasadena, California. She holds a bachelor's degree in Business Administration from Robert Morris College (Pennsylvania), a master's degree in Business from Northern Illinois University, and a doctorate in Adult and Community Education from Ball State University. Before joining Pasadena City College, she spent 12 years in the computer industry where she was a systems analyst, sales representative, and Director of Customer Education with Unisys Corporation. She also worked for Ernst & Young on the development of large systems applications for their clients. She has written and developed training materials for custom systems applications in both the public and private sector, and has written and edited numerous computer application textbooks.

This book is dedicated to my students, who inspire me every day.

Robert L. Ferrett recently retired as the Director of the Center for Instructional Computing at Eastern Michigan University, where he provided computer training and support to faculty. He has authored or co-authored more than 70 books on Access, PowerPoint, Excel, Publisher, WordPerfect, Windows, Word, OpenOffice, and Computer Fundamentals. He has been designing, developing, and delivering computer workshops for more than three decades. Before writing for the *GO! Series*, Bob was a series editor for the Learn Series. He has a bachelor's degree in Psychology, a master's degree in Geography, and a master's degree in Interdisciplinary Technology from Eastern Michigan University. His doctoral studies were in Instructional Technology at Wayne State University.

I'd like to dedicate this book to my wife Mary Jane,
whose constant support has been so important all these years.

Teach the Course You Want in Less Time

A Microsoft® Office textbook designed for student success!

GO!

- **Project-Based –** Students learn by creating projects that they will use in the real world.
- **Microsoft Procedural Syntax –** Steps are written to put students in the right place at the right time.
- **Teachable Moment –** Expository text is woven into the steps—at the moment students need to know it—not chunked together in a block of text that will go unread.
- **Sequential Pagination –** Students have actual page numbers instead of confusing letters and abbreviations.

Student Outcomes and Learning Objectives – Objectives are clustered around projects that result in student outcomes.

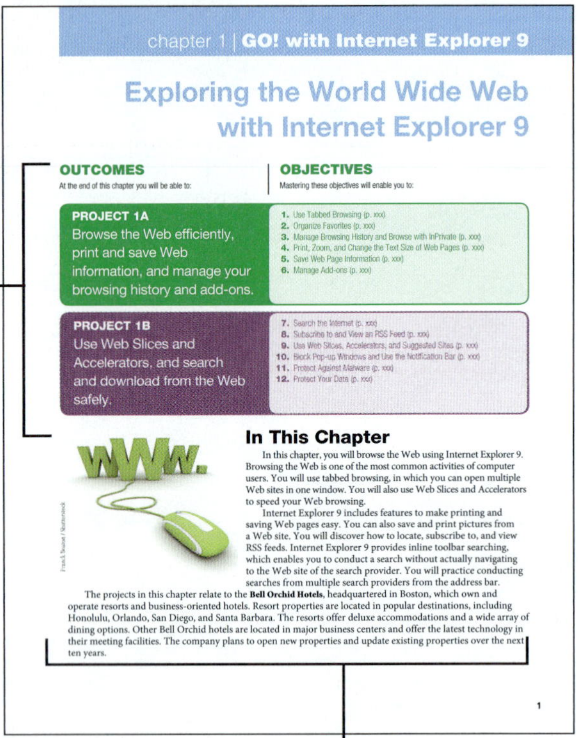

chapter 1 | GO! with Internet Explorer 9

Exploring the World Wide Web with Internet Explorer 9

OUTCOMES
At the end of this chapter you will be able to:

OBJECTIVES
Mastering these objectives will enable you to:

PROJECT 1A
Browse the Web efficiently, print and save Web information, and manage your browsing history and add-ons.

1. Use Tabbed Browsing (p. xxx)
2. Organize Favorites (p. xxx)
3. Manage Browsing History and Browse with InPrivate (p. xxx)
4. Print, Zoom, and Change the Text Size of Web Pages (p. xxx)
5. Save Web Page Information (p. xxx)
6. Manage Add-ons (p. xxx)

PROJECT 1B
Use Web Slices and Accelerators, and search and download from the Web safely.

7. Search the Internet (p. xxx)
8. Subscribe to and View an RSS Feed (p. xxx)
9. Use Web Slices, Accelerators, and Suggested Sites (p. xxx)
10. Block Pop-up Windows and Use the Notification Bar (p. xxx)
11. Protect Against Malware (p. xxx)
12. Protect Your Data (p. xxx)

In This Chapter

In this chapter, you will browse the Web using Internet Explorer 9. Browsing the Web is one of the most common activities of computer users. You will use tabbed browsing, in which you can open multiple Web sites in one window. You will also use Web Slices and Accelerators to speed your Web browsing.

Internet Explorer 9 includes features to make printing and saving Web pages easy. You can also save and print pictures from a Web site. You will discover how to locate, subscribe to, and view RSS feeds. Internet Explorer 9 provides inline toolbar searching, which enables you to conduct a search without actually navigating to the Web site of the search provider. You will practice conducting searches from multiple search providers from the address bar.

The projects in this chapter relate to the **Bell Orchid Hotels**, headquartered in Boston, which own and operate resorts and business-oriented hotels. Resort properties are located in popular destinations, including Honolulu, Orlando, San Diego, and Santa Barbara. The resorts offer deluxe accommodations and a wide array of dining options. Other Bell Orchid hotels are located in major business centers and offer the latest technology in their meeting facilities. The company plans to open new properties and update existing properties over the next ten years.

1

Project Activities – A project summary stated clearly and quickly.

Project Files – Clearly shows students which files are needed for the project and the names they will use to save their documents.

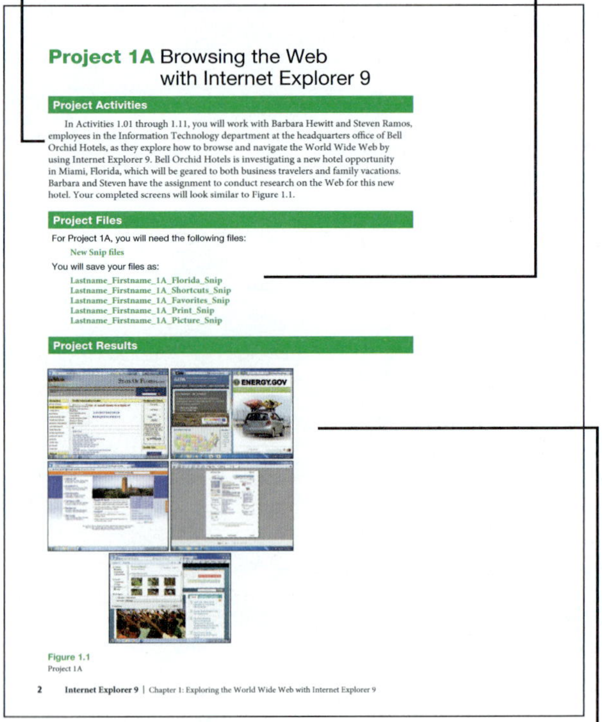

Project 1A Browsing the Web with Internet Explorer 9

Project Activities

In Activities 1.01 through 1.11, you will work with Barbara Hewitt and Steven Ramos, employees in the Information Technology department at the headquarters office of Bell Orchid Hotels, as they explore how to browse and navigate the World Wide Web by using Internet Explorer 9. Bell Orchid Hotels is investigating a new hotel opportunity in Miami, Florida, which will be geared to both business travelers and family vacations. Barbara and Steven have the assignment to conduct research on the Web for this new hotel. Your completed screens will look similar to Figure 1.1.

Project Files

For Project 1A, you will need the following files:

New Snip files

You will save your files as:

Lastname_Firstname_1A_Florida_Snip
Lastname_Firstname_1A_Shortcuts_Snip
Lastname_Firstname_1A_Favorites_Snip
Lastname_Firstname_1A_Print_Snip
Lastname_Firstname_1A_Picture_Snip

Project Results

Figure 1.1
Project 1A

2 Internet Explorer 9 | Chapter 1: Exploring the World Wide Web with Internet Explorer 9

Scenario – Each chapter opens with a story that sets the stage for the projects the student will create.

Project Results – Shows students how their final outcome will appear.

Key Feature

Microsoft Procedural Syntax – Steps are written to put the student in the right place at the right time.

Color Coding – Color variations between the two projects in each chapter make it easy to identify which project students are working on.

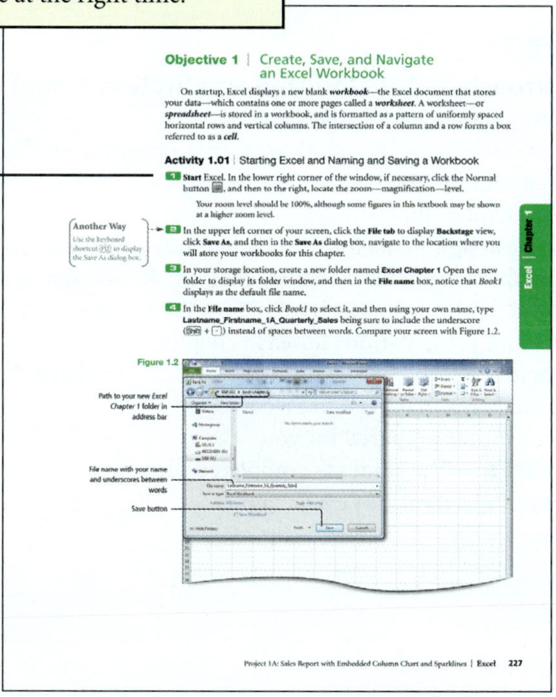
Objective 1 | Create, Save, and Navigate an Excel Workbook

On startup, Excel displays a new blank *workbook*—the Excel document that stores your data—which contains one or more pages called a *worksheet*. A worksheet—or *spreadsheet*—is stored in a workbook, and is formatted as a pattern of uniformly spaced horizontal rows and vertical columns. The intersection of a column and a row forms a box referred to as a *cell*.

Activity 1.01 | Starting Excel and Naming and Saving a Workbook

1. **Start** Excel. In the lower right corner of the window, if necessary, click the Normal button, and then to the right, locate the zoom—magnification—level.

   Your zoom level should be 100%, although some figures in this textbook may be shown at a higher zoom level.

2. In the upper left corner of your screen, click the **File tab** to display **Backstage** view, click **Save As**, and then in the **Save As** dialog box, navigate to the location where you will store your workbooks for this chapter.

3. In your storage location, create a new folder named **Excel Chapter 1** Open the new folder to display its folder window, and then in the **File name** box, notice that *Book1* displays as the default file name.

4. In the **File name** box, click *Book1* to select it, and then using your own name, type **Lastname_Firstname_1A_Quarterly_Sales** being sure to include the underscore (Shift + -) instead of spaces between words. Compare your screen with Figure 1.2.

Another Way: Use the keyboard shortcut F12 to display the Save As dialog box.

Figure 1.2

Excel | Chapter 1

Project 1A: Sales Report with Embedded Column Chart and Sparklines | Excel 227

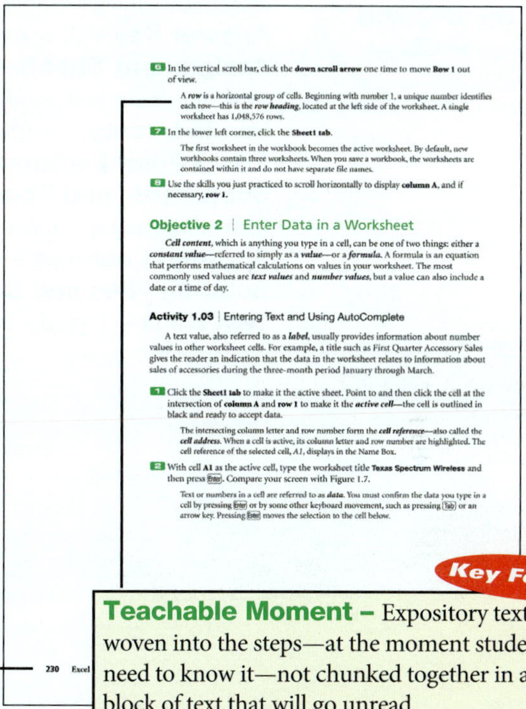
6. In the vertical scroll bar, click the **down scroll arrow** one time to move **Row 1** out of view.

   A *row* is a horizontal group of cells. Beginning with number 1, a unique number identifies each row—this is the *row heading*, located at the left side of the worksheet. A single worksheet has 1,048,576 rows.

7. In the lower left corner, click the **Sheet1 tab**.

   The first worksheet in the workbook becomes the active worksheet. By default, new workbooks contain three worksheets. When you save a workbook, the worksheets are contained within it and do not have separate file names.

8. Use the skills you just practiced to scroll horizontally to display **column A**, and if necessary, **row 1**.

Objective 2 | Enter Data in a Worksheet

Cell content, which is anything you type in a cell, can be one of two things: either a *constant value*—referred to simply as a *value*—or a *formula*. A formula is an equation that performs mathematical calculations on values in your worksheet. The most commonly used values are *text values* and *number values*, but a value can also include a date or a time of day.

Activity 1.03 | Entering Text and Using AutoComplete

A text value, also referred to as a *label*, usually provides information about number values in other worksheet cells. For example, a title such as First Quarter Accessory Sales gives the reader an indication that the data in the worksheet relates to information about sales of accessories during the three-month period January through March.

1. Click the **Sheet1 tab** to make it the active sheet. Point to and then click the cell at the intersection of **column A** and **row 1** to make it the *active cell*—the cell is outlined in black and ready to accept data.

   The intersecting column letter and row number form the *cell reference*—also called the *cell address*. When a cell is active, its column letter and row number are highlighted. The cell reference of the selected cell, *A1*, displays in the Name Box.

2. With cell **A1** as the active cell, type the worksheet title **Texas Spectrum Wireless** and then press Enter. Compare your screen with Figure 1.7.

   Text or numbers in a cell are referred to as *data*. You must confirm the data you type in a cell by pressing Enter or by some other keyboard movement, such as pressing Tab or an arrow key. Pressing Enter moves the selection to the cell below.

230 Excel

Key Feature

Sequential Pagination – Students are given actual page numbers to navigate through the textbook instead of confusing letters and abbreviations.

Key Feature

Teachable Moment – Expository text is woven into the steps—at the moment students need to know it—not chunked together in a block of text that will go unread.

End-of-Chapter

Content-Based Assessments – Assessments with defined solutions.

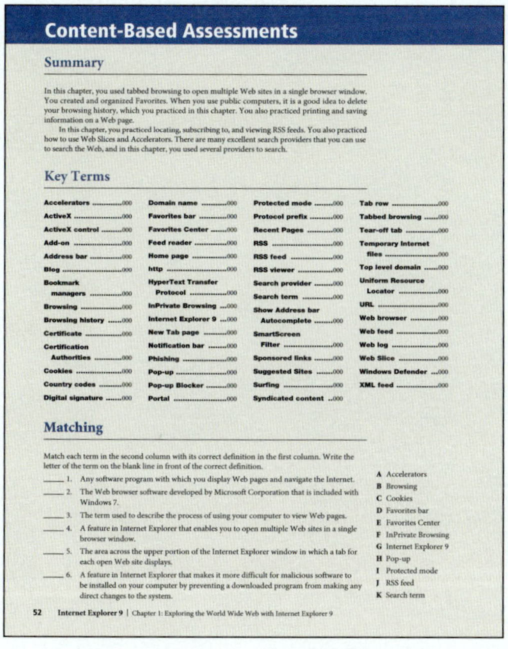
Content-Based Assessments

Summary

In this chapter, you used tabbed browsing to open multiple Web sites in a single browser window. You created and organized Favorites. When you use public computers, it is a good idea to delete your browsing history, which you practiced in this chapter. You also practiced printing and saving information on a Web page.

In this chapter, you practiced locating, subscribing to, and viewing RSS feeds. You also practiced how to use Web Slices and Accelerators. There are many excellent search providers that you can use to search the Web, and in this chapter, you used several providers to search.

Key Terms

Accelerators 000, ActiveX 000, ActiveX control 000, Add-on 000, Address bar 000, Blog 000, Bookmark managers 000, Browsing 000, Browsing history 000, Certificate 000, Certification Authorities 000, Cookies 000, Country codes 000, Digital signature 000, Domain name 000, Favorites bar 000, Favorites Center 000, Feed reader 000, Home page 000, http 000, HyperText Transfer Protocol 000, InPrivate Browsing 000, Internet Explorer 9 000, New Tab page 000, Notification bar 000, Phishing 000, Pop-up 000, Pop-up Blocker 000, Portal 000, Protected mode 000, Protocol prefix 000, Recent Pages 000, RSS 000, RSS feed 000, RSS viewer 000, Search provider 000, Search term 000, Show Address bar Autocomplete 000, SmartScreen Filter 000, Sponsored links 000, Suggested Sites 000, Surfing 000, Syndicated content 000, Tab row 000, Tabbed browsing 000, Tear-off tab 000, Temporary Internet files 000, Top level domain 000, Uniform Resource Locator 000, URL 000, Web browser 000, Web feed 000, Web log 000, Web Slice 000, Windows Defender 000, XML feed 000

Matching

Match each term in the second column with its correct definition in the first column. Write the letter of the term on the blank line in front of the correct definition.

___ 1. Any software program with which you display Web pages and navigate the Internet.
___ 2. The Web browser software developed by Microsoft Corporation that is included with Windows 7.
___ 3. The term used to describe the process of using your computer to view Web pages.
___ 4. A feature in Internet Explorer that enables you to open multiple Web sites in a single browser window.
___ 5. The area across the upper portion of the Internet Explorer window in which a tab for each open Web site displays.
___ 6. A feature in Internet Explorer that makes it more difficult for malicious software to be installed on your computer by preventing a downloaded program from making any direct changes to the system.

A Accelerators
B Browsing
C Cookies
D Favorites bar
E Favorites Center
F InPrivate Browsing
G Internet Explorer 9
H Pop-up
I Protected mode
J RSS feed
K Search term

52 Internet Explorer 9 | Chapter 1: Exploring the World Wide Web with Internet Explorer 9

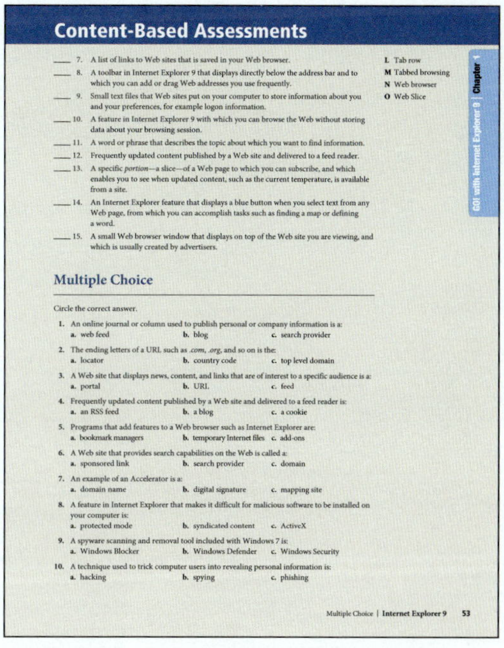
Content-Based Assessments

___ 7. A list of links to Web sites that is saved in your Web browser.
___ 8. A toolbar in Internet Explorer 9 that displays directly below the address bar and to which you can add or drag Web addresses you use frequently.
___ 9. Small text files that Web sites put on your computer to store information about you and your preferences, for example logon information.
___ 10. A feature in Internet Explorer 9 with which you can browse the Web without storing data about your browsing session.
___ 11. A word or phrase that describes the topic about which you want to find information.
___ 12. Frequently updated content published by a Web site and delivered to a feed reader.
___ 13. A specific portion—a slice—of a Web page to which you can subscribe, and which enables you to see when updated content, such as the current temperature, is available from a site.
___ 14. An Internet Explorer feature that displays a blue button when you select text from any Web page, from which you can accomplish tasks such as finding a map or defining a word.
___ 15. A small Web browser window that displays on top of the Web site you are viewing, and which is usually created by advertisers.

L Tab row
M Tabbed browsing
N Web browser
O Web Slice

Multiple Choice

Circle the correct answer.

1. An online journal or column used to publish personal or company information is a:
   a. web feed b. blog c. search provider
2. The ending letters of a URL such as .com, .org, and so on is the:
   a. locator b. country code c. top level domain
3. A Web site that displays news, content, and links that are of interest to a specific audience is a:
   a. portal b. URL c. feed
4. Frequently updated content published by a Web site and delivered to a feed reader is:
   a. an RSS feed b. a blog c. a cookie
5. Programs that add features to a Web browser such as Internet Explorer are:
   a. bookmark managers b. temporary Internet files c. add-ons
6. A Web site that provides search capabilities on the Web is called a:
   a. sponsored link b. search provider c. domain
7. An example of an Accelerator is a:
   a. domain name b. digital signature c. mapping site
8. A feature in Internet Explorer that makes it difficult for malicious software to be installed on your computer is:
   a. protected mode b. syndicated content c. ActiveX
9. A spyware scanning and removal tool included with Windows 7 is:
   a. Windows Blocker b. Windows Defender c. Windows Security
10. A technique used to trick computer users into revealing personal information is:
   a. hacking b. spying c. phishing

GO! with Internet Explorer 9 | Chapter 1

Multiple Choice | Internet Explorer 9 53

Student Resources

Companion Website – Student Data Files, the Online Study Guide (an interactive quiz), and a Glossary are at www.pearsonhighered.com/go.

All Instructor materials available on the IRC and IRCD

Instructor Resources

Additional Project Exams (formerly Point-Counted Production Tests) – provided by chapter, application, and project with a scorecard for easy grading.

Annotated Solution Files – Coupled with the scorecards, these create a grading and scoring system that makes grading so much easier for you.

Answer Key – Answers to end-of-chapter questions.

Assignment Sheets – Lists all the assignments for the chapter. Just add in the course information, due dates, and points. Providing these to students ensures they will know what is due and when.

Image Library – A library of all the figures from the book.

PowerPoint Lectures – PowerPoint presentations for each chapter.

Scorecards and Scoring Rubrics – Can be used by either students to check their work or by instructors as a quick check-off for the items that need to be corrected.

Scripted Lectures – Classroom lectures prepared for you.

Solution Files and Solution PDFs – The student's completed file.

Test Bank – Includes a variety of test questions for each chapter.

Exploring the World Wide Web with Internet Explorer 9

OUTCOMES

At the end of this chapter you will be able to:

OBJECTIVES

Mastering these objectives will enable you to:

PROJECT 1A

Browse the Web efficiently, print and save Web information, and manage your browsing history and add-ons.

1. Use Tabbed Browsing (p. 3)
2. Organize Favorites (p. 15)
3. Manage Browsing History and Browse with InPrivate (p. 20)
4. Print, Zoom, and Change the Text Size of Web Pages (p. 24)
5. Save Web Page Information (p. 28)
6. Manage Add-ons (p. 31)

PROJECT 1B

Use Web Slices and Accelerators, and search and download from the Web safely.

7. Search the Internet (p. 35)
8. Subscribe to and View an RSS Feed (p. 37)
9. Use Web Slices, Accelerators, and Suggested Sites (p. 41)
10. Block Pop-up Windows and Use the Notification Bar (p. 46)
11. Protect Against Malware (p. 47)
12. Protect Your Data (p. 49)

Franck Boston / Shutterstock

In This Chapter

In this chapter, you will browse the Web using Internet Explorer 9. Browsing the Web is one of the most common activities of computer users. You will use tabbed browsing, in which you can open multiple Web sites in one window. You will also use Web Slices and Accelerators to speed your Web browsing.

Internet Explorer 9 includes features to make printing and saving Web pages easy. You can also save and print pictures from a Web site. You will discover how to locate, subscribe to, and view RSS feeds. Internet Explorer 9 provides inline toolbar searching, which enables you to conduct a search without actually navigating to the Web site of the search provider. You will practice conducting searches from multiple search providers from the address bar.

The projects in this chapter relate to the **Bell Orchid Hotels**, headquartered in Boston, which own and operate resorts and business-oriented hotels. Resort properties are located in popular destinations, including Honolulu, Orlando, San Diego, and Santa Barbara. The resorts offer deluxe accommodations and a wide array of dining options. Other Bell Orchid hotels are located in major business centers and offer the latest technology in their meeting facilities. The company plans to open new properties and update existing properties over the next ten years.

Project 1A Browsing the Web with Internet Explorer 9

Project Activities

In Activities 1.01 through 1.11, you will work with Barbara Hewitt and Steven Ramos, employees in the Information Technology department at the headquarters of Bell Orchid Hotels, as they explore how to browse and navigate the World Wide Web by using Internet Explorer 9. Barbara and Steven will conduct research on the Web for new hotels in Miami and Pasadena, including information on weather, transportation, economic development assistance, and educational opportunities for staff. Your completed screens will look similar to Figure 1.1.

Project Files

For Project 1A, you will need the following files:

New Snip files

You will save your files as:

Lastname_Firstname_1A_Census_Snip
Lastname_Firstname_1A_Shortcuts_Snip
Lastname_Firstname_1A_Favorites_Snip
Lastname_Firstname_1A_Print_Snip
Lastname_Firstname_1A_Picture_Snip

Project Results

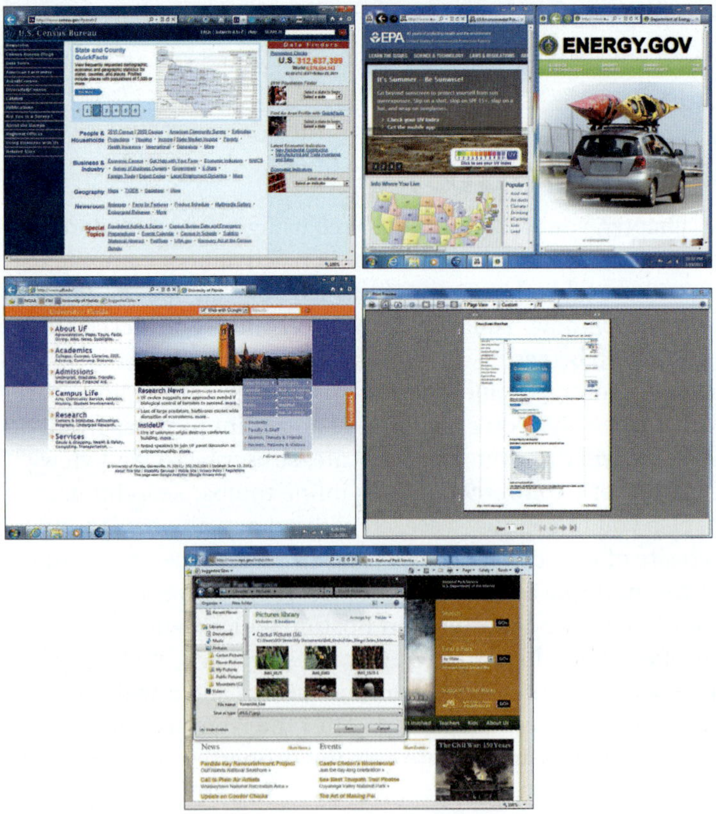

Figure 1.1
Project 1A

Objective 1 | Use Tabbed Browsing

A ***Web browser*** is a software program that you use to display Web pages and navigate the Internet. ***Internet Explorer 9*** is the Web browser software developed by Microsoft Corporation. ***Browsing*** is the term used to describe the process of using your computer to find and view Web pages. ***Surfing*** refers to the process of navigating the Internet either for a particular item or for anything that is of interest, and quickly moving from one item to another.

Browsing the Web is one of the most common activities performed by individuals who use computers. Common tasks that you perform on the Internet might include looking at your favorite news sites, managing your finances with your bank, conducting research, shopping, sending e-mail, using social media sites such as Facebook or Twitter, or reading or writing entries in a ***blog***. A blog—short for ***Web log***—is an online journal or column used to publish personal or company information in an informal manner. For example, the developers of Microsoft Word maintain a blog of information about using Word at *http://blogs.office.com/b/microsoft-word.*

Activity 1.01 | Using Tabbed Browsing

Tabbed browsing is a feature in Internet Explorer that enables you to open multiple Web sites in a single browser window. You open each new Web page in a new tab, and then switch among your open Web pages by clicking the tab that displays in the upper portion of the screen.

In this activity, you will work with Barbara and Steven, who are conducting research on new hotels.

Another Way

On the Start menu, in the Search box, type Internet Explorer, and then click the program name.

1 Insert a USB flash drive into your computer for use later, and then in the **AutoPlay** dialog box that displays, in the upper right corner, click the red **Close** button. On the taskbar, click the **Internet Explorer** button. If an Add-ons bar displays near the bottom of the screen, on the right, click **Ask me later**. If the Internet Explorer window does not fill the screen, on the right side of the title bar, click the **Maximize** button. If the status bar does not display at the bottom of the window, right-click in the title bar, and then click Status bar.

The ***home page*** that is set on your computer displays. On your computer, *home page* refers to whatever Web page or pages you have selected—or is set by default—to display on your computer when you start Internet Explorer. When visiting a Web site, *home page* refers to the starting point for the remainder of the pages on that site.

For example, your computer manufacturer may have set its company site as the default home page. At your college, the home page of your college's Web site might be the home page on the computer at which you are working.

2 At the top of your screen, click in the **address bar** to select (highlight) the current Web address, point to a link on the page, and then compare your screen with Figure 1.2. Take a moment to study the parts of the Internet Explorer window in the table in Figure 1.3.

The ***address bar*** is the area at the top of the Internet Explorer window that displays, and where you can type, a ***URL—Uniform Resource Locator***—which is an address that uniquely identifies a location on the Internet. You can also search using the address bar.

A URL is usually preceded by *http://* and can contain additional details, such as the name of a page of hypertext, which often has the extension *.html* or *.htm*.

Figure 1.2

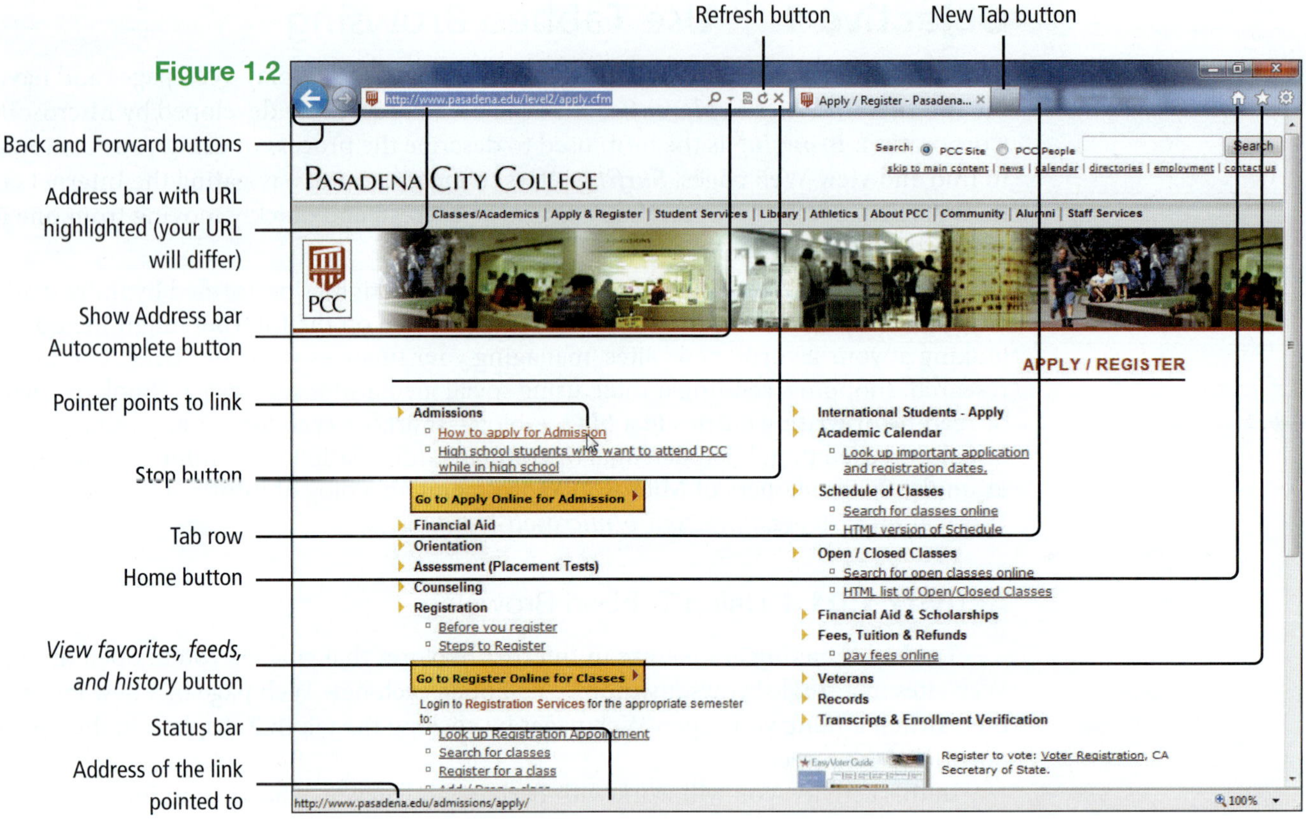

Parts of the Internet Explorer Window

Window Element	Function
Address bar	Displays the URL of the currently active Web page; it is also used to enter search terms.
Back and Forward buttons	Display Web pages you have previously visited.
View favorites, feeds, and history button	Opens the Favorites Center pane, which is an area to manage your Favorites, browser history, and subscribed RSS feeds.
New Tab button	Opens a new tab.
Home button	Takes you to your default home page.
Show Address bar Autocomplete button	Displays a list of recently visited Web sites.
Refresh button	Updates the content of the displayed Web page; for example, to update temperatures on a weather site or update stock prices on a financial site.
Status bar	Displays, on the left, the URL for a link to which your mouse is pointing; on the right, displays information about the download process of a Web site and also icons to change your Zoom level.
Stop button	Stops the download of a Web page that you requested.
Tab row	Displays a tab for each open Web page.

Figure 1.3

Another Way

Instead of pressing Enter, you can click the small blue arrow at the end of the address bar.

3 In the **address bar**, with the current URL selected, type **www.usa.gov** and then press Enter. Notice the URL in the **address bar**, and then compare your screen with Figure 1.4.

The Web site for the United States Government displays. By typing in the address bar, the new URL opens and the original URL—whatever your home page site was—closes.

A URL contains the ***protocol prefix***—in this instance ***http***—which stands for ***HyperText Transfer Protocol***. HTTP represents the set of communication rules used by your computer to connect to servers on the Web. Internet Explorer defaults to the *http* prefix, so it is not necessary to type it, even though it is part of the URL for this site. The protocol prefix is followed by a colon and the separators //.

A URL also contains the ***domain name***—in this instance *www.usa.gov*. A domain name is an organization's unique name on the Internet, and consists of a chosen name combined with a ***top level domain*** such as *.com* or *.org* or *.gov*.

Figure 1.4

Alert! | Web Sites Update Content Frequently

As you progress through the projects in this chapter, the pictures of various Web sites in this textbook may not match your screens exactly, because Web site administrators frequently update content. This will not affect your ability to complete the projects successfully.

4 Take a moment to study the table in Figure 1.5 to become familiar with top level domains.

There are two types of top level domains—the generic top level domains, such as *.com*, *.org*, and so on (shown in Figure 1.5), and the ***country codes*** such as *.ca* for Canada, *.cn* for China, and *.uk* for United Kingdom.

Common Domain Name Extensions and Organization Types

Domain Name Extension	Organization Type
.com	Commercial businesses and companies
.co	Commercial businesses and companies
.net	Internet service providers and other communications-oriented organizations
.org	Usually nonprofit organizations
.edu	U.S. educational only
.gov	U.S. government only
.info	Information services
.mobi	Mobile devices
.name	Individuals and families
.biz	Usually small businesses

Figure 1.5

5 Click in the **address bar** to select the URL text, and then type **epa.gov** and press Enter.

The acronym *www*, which stands for *World Wide Web*, is used for uniformity on the Web. You can usually omit typing *www* and its following dot, because most Web servers are configured to handle a URL with or without it. If a Web page does not display without typing *www*, retype the URL and include *www*.

6 To the right of the **URL**, locate and click the **Show Address bar Autocomplete** button. Compare your screen with Figure 1.6.

The ***Show Address bar Autocomplete*** button displays a list of recently accessed locations. By clicking an item on this list, you can jump to a recently accessed location quickly.

Figure 1.6

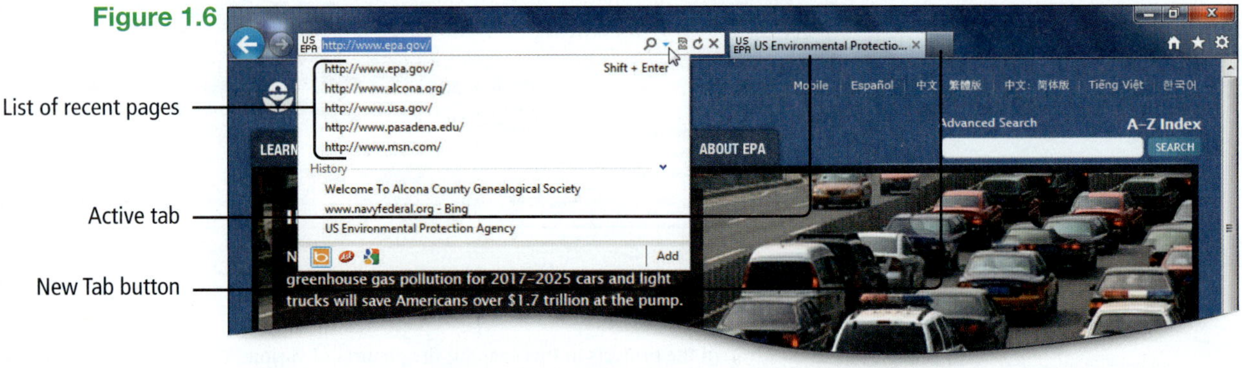

7 Click the **Show Address bar Autocomplete** button again to close the list, and then locate and point to the **New Tab** button, which is to the immediate right of the **US Environmental Protection Agency tab**. Click the **New Tab** button one time. Compare your screen with Figure 1.7.

The ***New Tab page*** displays, and in the address bar, *about:Tabs* is selected. This *What do you want to do next?* page will display a list of sites that you have visited frequently, which is useful if you want to open a favorite site.

Figure 1.7

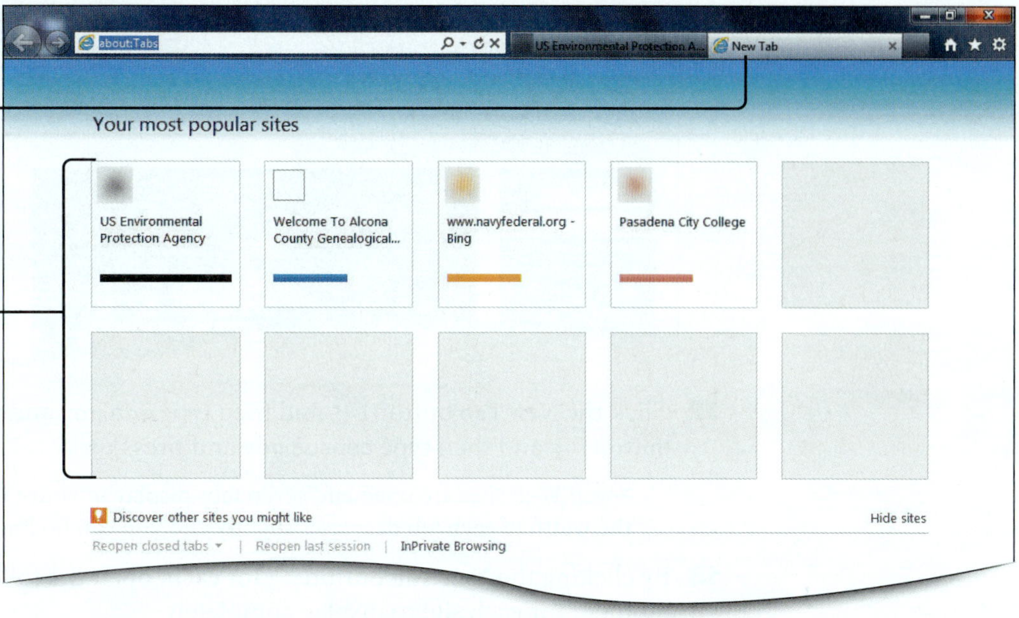

8 With the text in the **address bar** selected, type **weather.gov** and then press Enter to display the Web site for the **National Weather Service**. Click the **New Tab** button, type **nps.gov** and then press Enter. Compare your screen with Figure 1.8.

The Web site for the National Park Service opens in the third tab.

Figure 1.8

9 On the **tab row**, click the first open tab—the **US EPA tab**.

The Web site for the Environmental Protection Agency redisplays. Recall that by opening multiple sites on tabs, you can switch between Web sites easily by clicking a tab.

10 On the taskbar, *point to* the **Internet Explorer** icon to display a thumbnail for each open tab.

Here you can see the Web sites that you have open in Internet Explorer, and can navigate to a site by clicking its thumbnail.

11 At the end of the **tab row**, click the **New Tab** button, type **commerce.gov** and then press Enter to display the site for the **US Department of Commerce**. Open another **New Tab**, type **noaa.gov** and then press Enter to display the site for the **National Oceanic and Atmospheric Administration**. Compare your screen with Figure 1.9.

Depending on the size of your screen and its resolution, the tabs might display differently than shown in Figure 1.9, but you can see that five Web pages are open.

Figure 1.9

12 Click the **New Tab** button, and then type **eda.gov** and press Enter. Click the **New Tab** button, and then type **census.gov** and press Enter.

Seven Web sites are open and seven tabs display in your tab row. As you open more tabs, the width of each tab decreases slightly and you can no longer read all the text on the tab.

13 By clicking the **New Tab** button for each, open the following five sites, waiting a moment for each site to display completely.

energystar.gov

www.dot.gov

www.bts.gov

florida.edu

mdc.edu

Twelve Web sites are open; however, on some screens Internet Explorer will display only nine or ten tabs in the tab row, plus the New Tab button. On larger screens, you might be able to display more tabs.

More Knowledge | Using the Address Bar Efficiently

The address bar, based on the first few characters that you type, will search across your History, Favorites, and RSS Feeds, displaying matches from the address or any part of the URL. When you see a match, you can click it to avoid retyping the entire URL of a site you have previously visited.

14 If displayed on your **tab row**, to the *left* of the first visible tab, click the **Scroll tab list backward** button, and then compare your screen with Figure 1.10.

When you have more sites open than Internet Explorer can display on the tab row, the small tabs with arrows indicate that more tabs are available. When the arrow is white, this indicates that additional tabs are open to the left or to the right. If the arrow is dimmed, no additional tabs are open in the direction of the arrow. If no arrows display, your screen is larger than what is shown in Figure 1.10 and can accommodate more tabs.

Figure 1.10

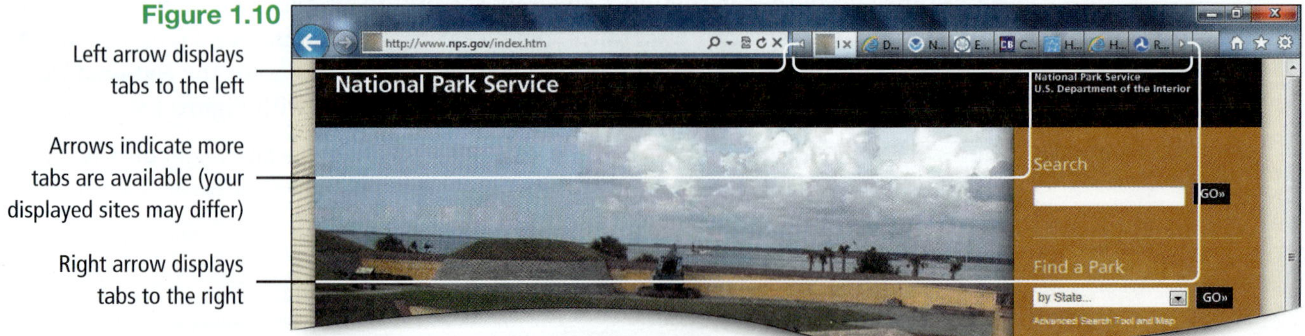

> **Alert! | Does your screen differ?**
>
> Your array of tabs may differ due to larger or smaller screen sizes or differing screen resolutions. If your screens do not match exactly, examine the figures shown. On a large screen, you may not see the Scroll tab list backward arrow.

Activity 1.02 | Using the Tab List, the Taskbar, and Shortcuts to Navigate Among Open Tabs

When you have multiple Web pages open at once, each one displays on a separate tab. When many Web pages are open and the width of each tab is decreased, it may become difficult to determine which tab represents a specific site. In this activity, you will practice various ways to navigate the open tabs to find the one you want easily.

1 On the right end of the **address bar**, click the **Show Address bar Autocomplete** button. Then, click the **History** arrow to expand the History list. Compare your screen with Figure 1.11.

When multiple tabs are open, the Web site name on each tab is truncated—cut short. By clicking the Show Address bar Autocomplete button, at the top you can see a list of the last five open Web sites, in the order they were opened. By clicking the History button, you can see a list of the last 20 Web sites you opened.

From this list, you can click a site to move to another tab, regardless of whether the tab is visible on the tab row.

Figure 1.11

Five most recently visited Web sites, in order

Show Address bar Autocomplete button

Last Web sites visited

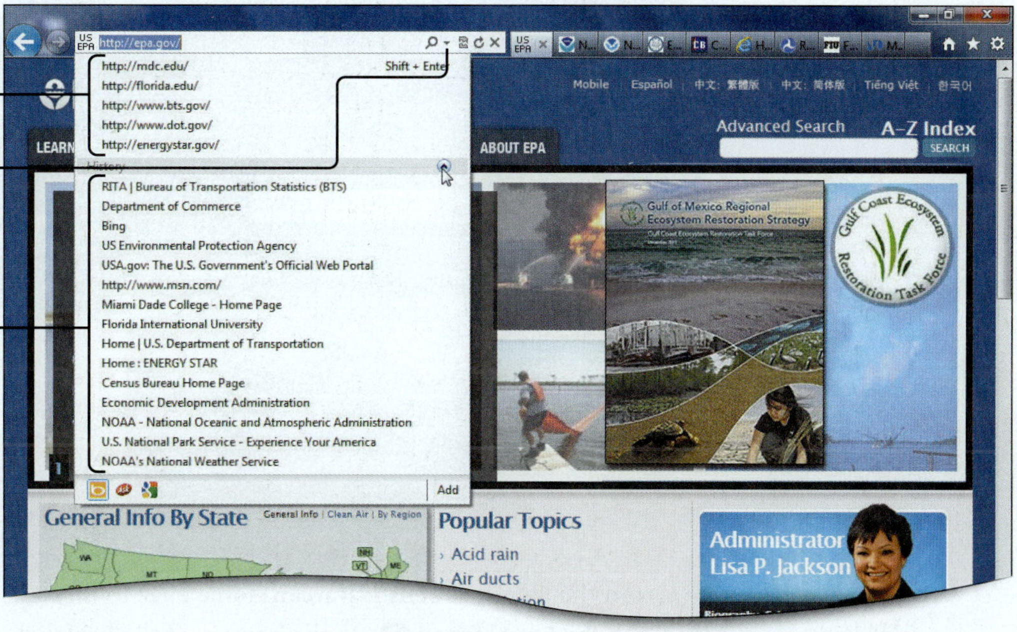

2 On the displayed list, under **History**, click **NOAA's National Weather Service**. Point to the **NOAA National Weather Service tab**, and then notice that a ScreenTip displays the site name and the site's URL. Notice also that because this is the active tab, the **Close Tab** button displays, as shown in Figure 1.12.

Figure 1.12

ScreenTip displays URL and site name of active tab

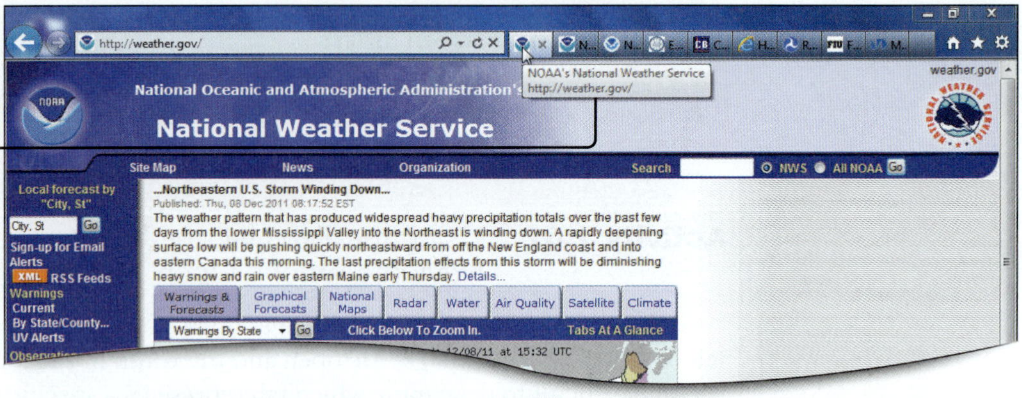

> **Another Way**
>
> Hold down Ctrl, and then press W to close the active tab.

3 On the **NOAA tab**, click the **Close Tab** button to close the **National Weather Service** Web site and to make the next tab in the row the active tab.

4 On the **taskbar**, *point* to the **Internet Explorer** button, and then compare your screen with Figure 1.13.

When you have a large number of Web pages open, a list showing the name of each open page displays, rather than a group of thumbnails. The number of open pages needed to change from thumbnails to a list varies with screen size and resolution.

Figure 1.13

List displays rather than thumbnails

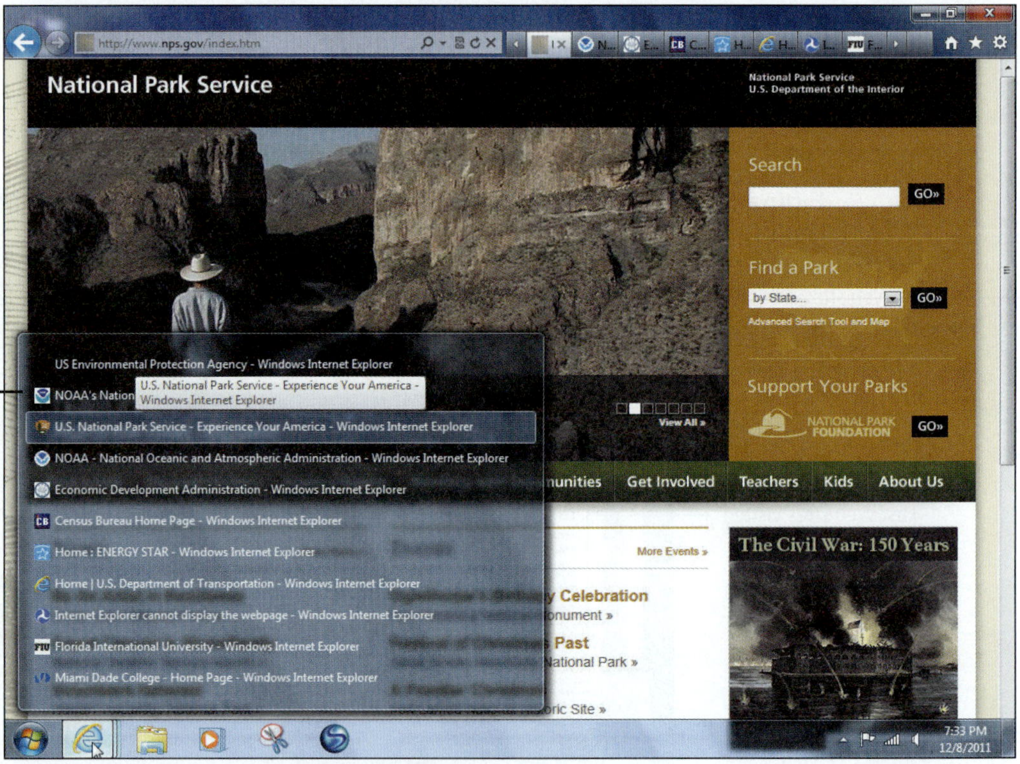

5 From the list, click **Census Bureau Home Page** to display its site.

6 Click the **Start** button. At the bottom of the list, click **All Programs**, and then click the **Accessories** folder. From the **Accessories** menu, click the **Snipping Tool** program. In the **Snipping Tool** dialog box, click the **New arrow**, and then click **Full-screen Snip**. In the **Snipping Tool** mark-up window, click the **Save Snip** button.

7 In the **Save As** dialog box, in the **navigation pane**, scroll down as necessary, and then under **Computer**, click your USB flash drive so that it displays in the **address bar**. On the toolbar, click the **New folder** button, type **IE9 Chapter 1** and then press Enter.

8 In the **file list**, double-click your **IE9 Chapter 1** folder to open it. Click in the **File name** box, and then replace the selected text by typing **Lastname_Firstname_1A_Census_Snip** Be sure the file type is **JPEG file**, and then press Enter. **Close** the **Snipping Tool** mark-up window. Hold this file until you finish Project 1A, and then submit this file as directed by your instructor.

9 On the **taskbar**, *point* to the **Internet Explorer** button again. Point to **Department of Commerce**. Notice that the link to the Department of Commerce Web site displays in the Internet Explorer window, and a Close button displays on the right side of the link. Compare your screen with Figure 1.14.

Figure 1.14

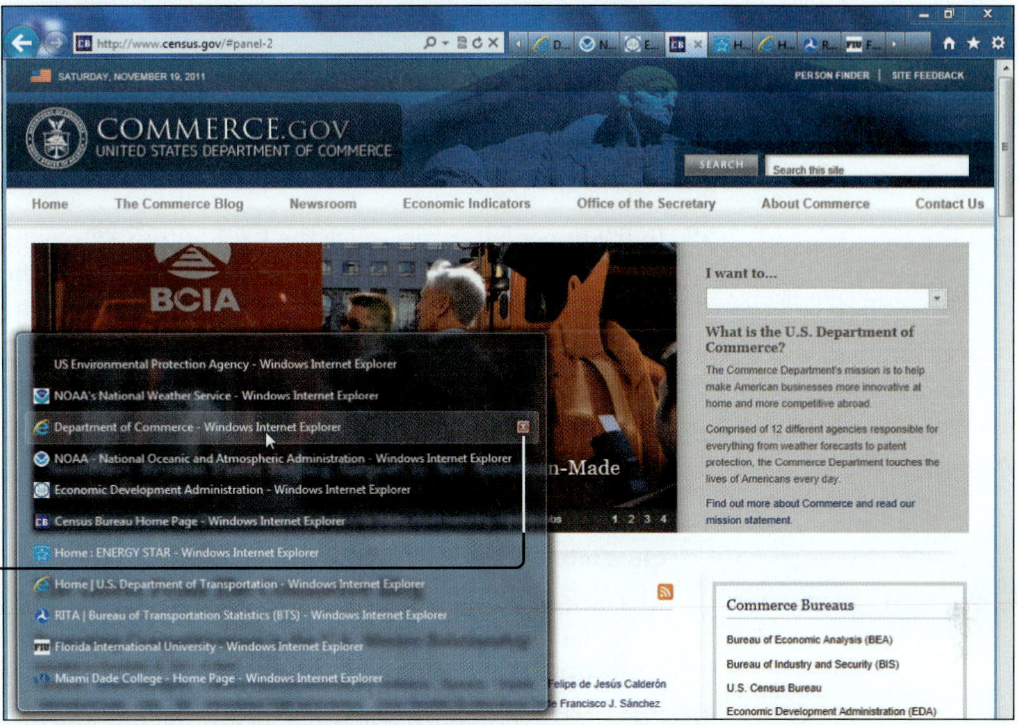

10 Click the **Close** button to close the Web page. *Except* for the **US Environmental Protection Agency** site and the **Economic Development Administration** site—do *not* close these two sites—use the same technique to close all the other sites. If necessary, click the **Economic Development Administration tab** to display the site. Compare your screen with Figure 1.15.

Although the content of this Web page may differ from what you currently have displayed, you can see that this Web page contains various links—other pages in this Web site that you can display. Groups of links are sometimes referred to as a ***navigation bar***.

Figure 1.15

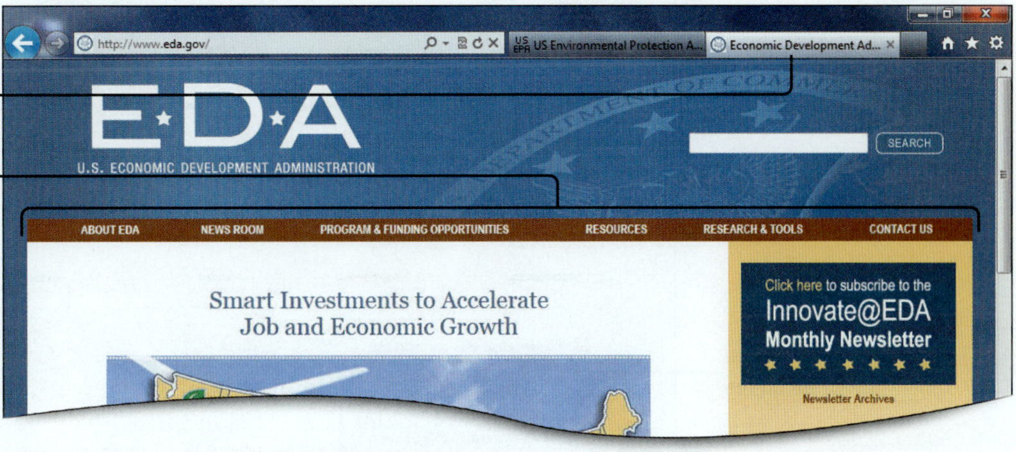

11 On the navigation bar near the top of the page, click **RESOURCES**; or, click any link on the page. Compare your screen with Figure 1.16.

When you click a link on a Web page, the new page typically opens on the same tab.

Figure 1.16

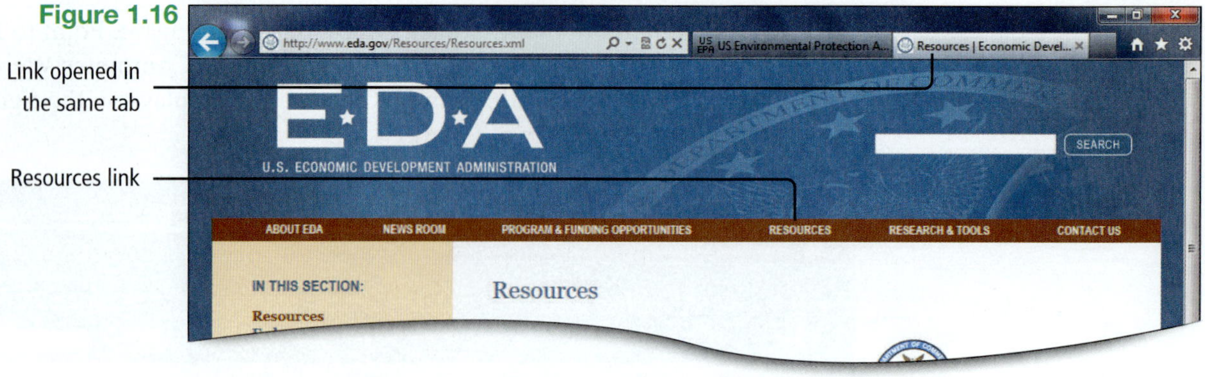

12 In the upper left corner, click the **Back** button one time to return to the previous page. Then, click the **Forward** button to redisplay the page regarding Resources information for the Economic Development Administration.

In this manner, you can click the Back and Forward buttons as necessary to redisplay pages you have visited.

13 Press Ctrl + T to open a new tab. Type **sunbiz.org** and press Enter. Press Ctrl + W to close the tab.

14 Point to the **US Environmental Protection Agency tab**, right-click, and then click **Close tab**.

Use this technique to close a tab without first making it the active tab. This is useful when you have some tabs open that you no longer need and want to close them quickly.

15 Press Ctrl + T to open a new tab. Below the thumbnails, click the **Reopen closed tabs arrow**, and then compare your screen with Figure 1.17.

After opening and closing sites, you can view thumbnails of popular sites, and a list of the sites you opened in this session. Then, if you want to do so, you can click a site name to open it on this tab.

Figure 1.17

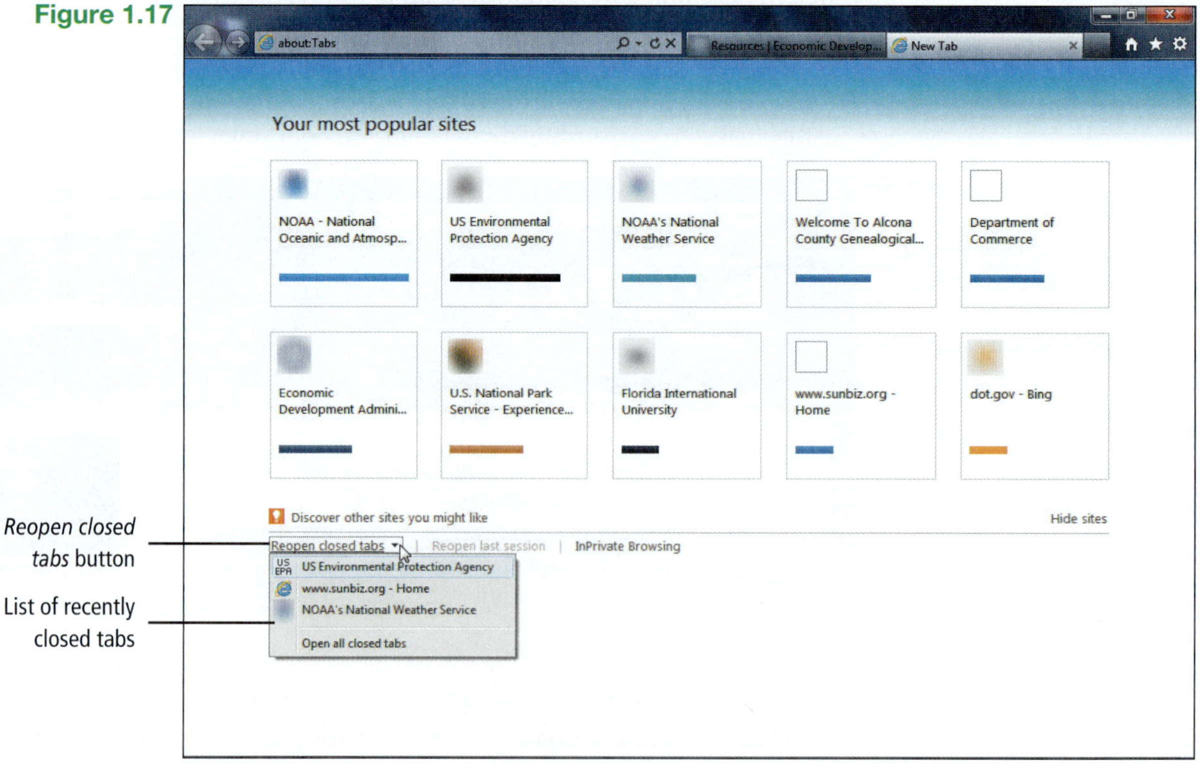

16 In the upper right corner of the Internet Explorer window, click the **Close** button.

When you close Internet Explorer, you are prompted to close all the tabs, or you can close only the current tab.

17 In the displayed **Internet Explorer** dialog box, click **Close all tabs**.

18 Take a moment to examine some additional shortcuts that you can use when navigating in Internet Explorer as shown in the table in Figure 1.18.

Keyboard and Mouse Shortcuts When Working with Tabs in Internet Explorer

To do this:	Press or do this:
Open a link on a page in a new tab in the background	Point to a link on a page and Ctrl + click; or point to the link, right-click, and click Open in new tab.
Open links in a new tab in the foreground	Ctrl + Shift + click using the left or middle mouse button.
Open a new tab in the foreground	Ctrl + T
Switch between tabs	Ctrl + Tab or Ctrl + Shift + Tab (right to left and left to right).
Close current tab (or current window when there are no open tabs)	Ctrl + W
Switch to a specific tab number	Ctrl + *n* (where *n* is a number between 1 and 8).
Switch to the last tab	Ctrl + 9.

Figure 1.18

Activity 1.03 | Using Tear-Off Tabs to View Tabs Side-By-Side and Create Shortcuts on the Taskbar

When you want to view the contents of two Web pages at the same time, you can use ***tear-off*** tabs to remove the tabs from the current Internet Explorer window and open them in new windows. You can also tear a tab off the tab bar and pin it to the taskbar to create a convenient shortcut to a site.

1 On the taskbar, click the **Internet Explorer** button. If an Add-ons bar displays, on the right, click **Ask me later**. If the Internet Explorer window does not fill the screen, on the right side of the title bar, click the **Maximize** button.

2 In the **address bar**, click one time, and then type **usa.gov** to open the *U.S. Government* site. Click the **New Tab** button and type **epa.gov** to open the *Environmental Protection Agency* site. Click the **New Tab** button and type **energy.gov** to open the *Department of Energy* site in a third tab.

3 Point to the **EPA tab**, drag the tab to the *left* until your pointer touches the left edge of the screen, and then release the mouse button. Notice that the *Environmental Protection Agency* page opens in a *new* window, and the window snaps to the left side of the screen. Compare your screen with Figure 1.19.

The original Internet Explorer window is still open, but now displays only two tabs. You now have two Internet Explorer windows open.

Figure 1.19

EPA site opens in a separate window

Two sites open in the original window

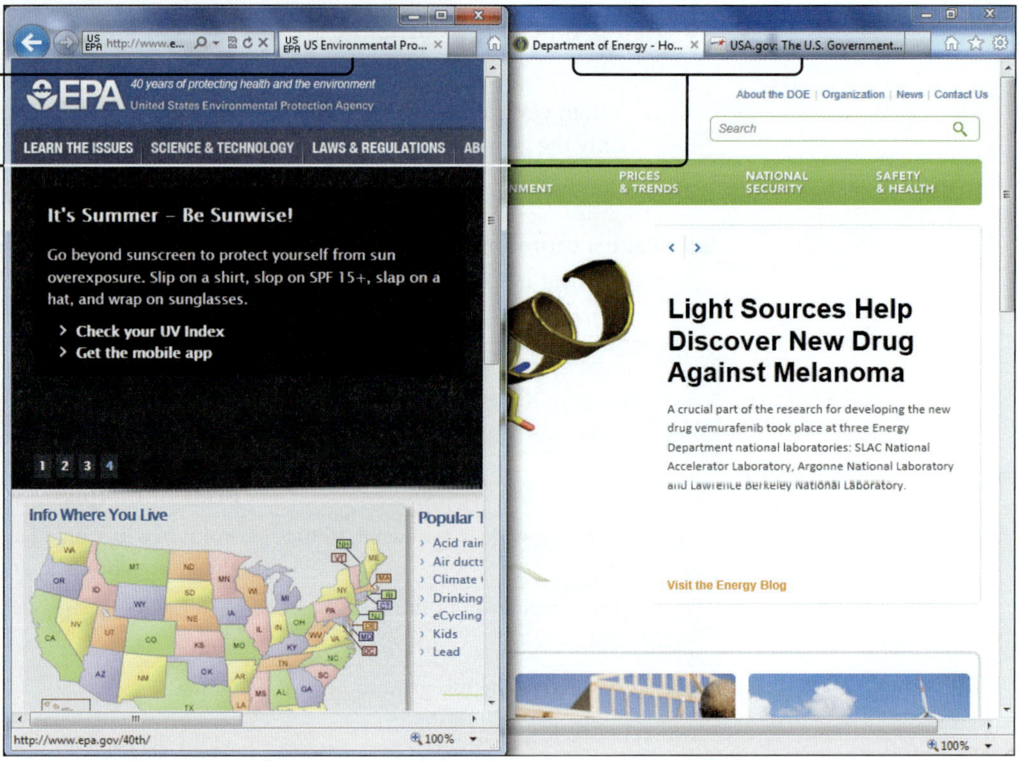

4 Point to the **Energy tab**, and then drag the tab to the right until the pointer touches the right edge of the screen. Notice that the *Department of Energy* page opens in a *new* window, and the window snaps to the right side of the screen. On the **taskbar**, point to the **Internet Explorer** button, and then click the **EPA window** to bring it to the front, as shown in Figure 1.20. Click on the **Energy window**, and notice that the red **Close** button [X] displays in the active window.

Figure 1.20

Each window occupies one-half of the screen

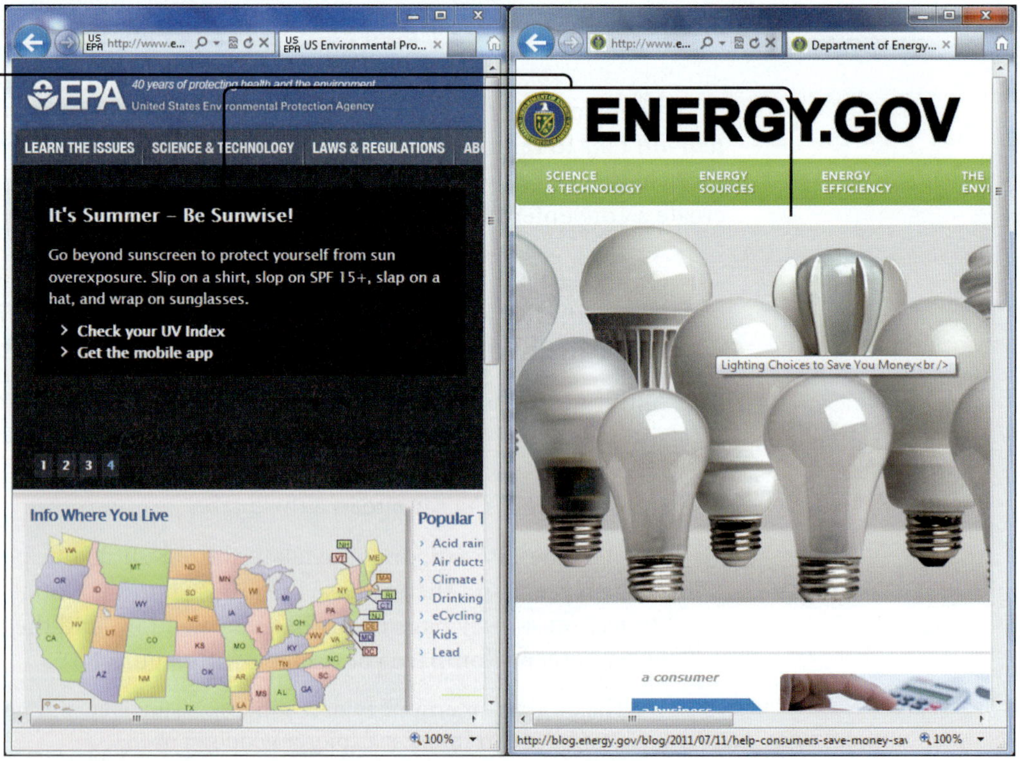

5 In the left window, drag the **EPA tab** down to the taskbar until a **Pin to Taskbar** ScreenTip displays, and then release the mouse button. If the window no longer covers the left half of the screen, point to the title bar and drag the window to the left until the pointer touches the left edge of the screen to snap it back into place.

6 Using the technique you just practiced, pin the **Energy tab** to the taskbar. If necessary, re-snap the window to the right side of the screen. Compare your screen with Figure 1.21.

Figure 1.21

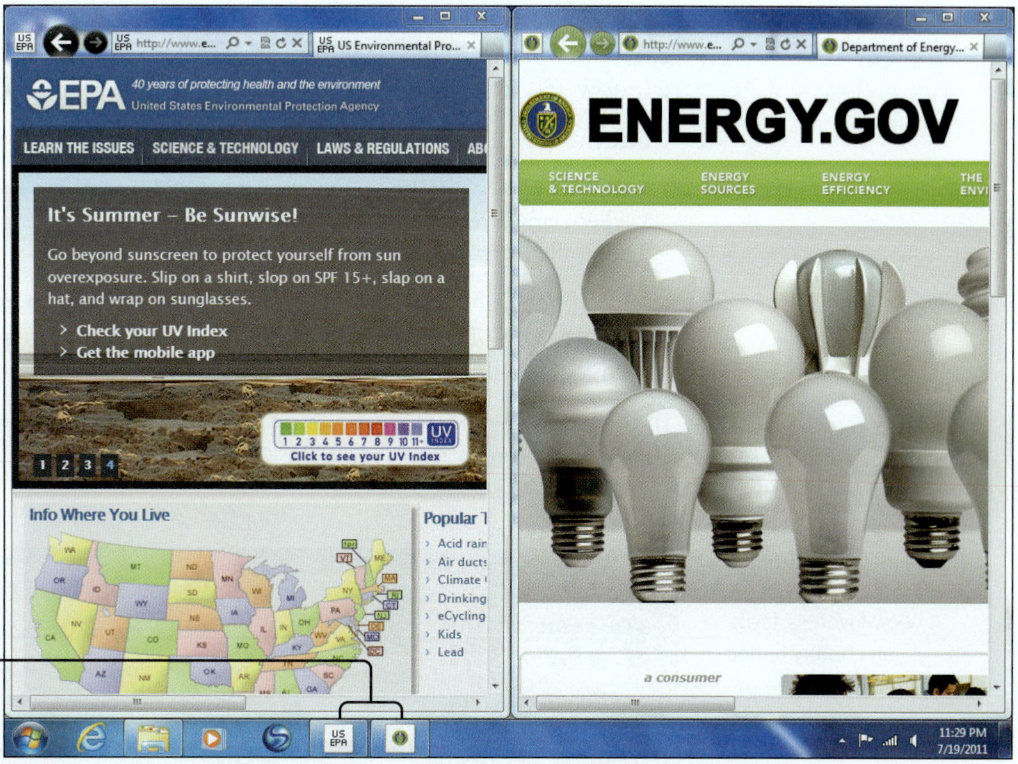

7 **Start** the **Snipping Tool** program, click the **New arrow**, and then click **Full-screen Snip**. In the **Snipping Tool** mark-up window, click the **Save Snip** button.

8 In the **Save As** dialog box, in the **navigation pane**, scroll down as necessary, and then under **Computer**, click your USB flash drive so that it displays in the **address bar**. Navigate to your **IE9 Chapter 1** folder, and then as the file name, type **Lastname_Firstname_1A_Shortcuts_Snip** Be sure the file type is **JPEG file**, and then press Enter. **Close** the **Snipping Tool** window. Hold this file until you finish Project 1A, and then submit this file as directed by your instructor.

9 **Close** all open windows. On the **taskbar**, right-click the **EPA** shortcut, and on the menu, click **Unpin this program from taskbar**. Use the same technique to unpin the **Energy** shortcut.

Objective 2 | Organize Favorites

The ***Favorites Center*** is a list of links to Web sites that you can save in your Web browser. Saving a Web site as a favorite enables you to return to it quickly. For example, if you have a favorite health site that you visit frequently, you can save the site's address as a Favorite. Returning to the site requires only one or two clicks instead of typing a complete URL.

You can create folders to organize your favorite links into groups that are meaningful to you. Then, you can either open one site from the folder, or open all the sites in the folder with a single click.

Activity 1.04 | Organizing Favorites and Creating a Favorites Folder

In this activity, you will help Barbara and Steven organize a group of sites that they believe will be useful to those who are conducting research for the new hotel in Miami.

1 **Close** any open windows and display your Windows 7 desktop. On the **taskbar**, click the **Internet Explorer** button, and then if necessary, Maximize the window. Click in the **address bar**, and then type **mdc.edu** and press Enter.

2 Click the **New Tab** button, type **florida.edu** and then press Enter.

Barbara and Steven know that managers will be looking for institutions of higher learning where employees can gain additional knowledge and credentials in management, computer science, and tourism management.

3 In the upper right corner, click the **View favorites, feeds, and history** button, and then at the top of the pane, to the right of *Add to favorites*, click the **arrow**. On the displayed list, click **Add current tabs to favorites**.

4 In the **Add Tabs to Favorites** dialog box, in the **Folder Name** box, type **Colleges and Universities** If necessary, click the Create in arrow and click Favorites. Compare your screen with Figure 1.22.

Figure 1.22

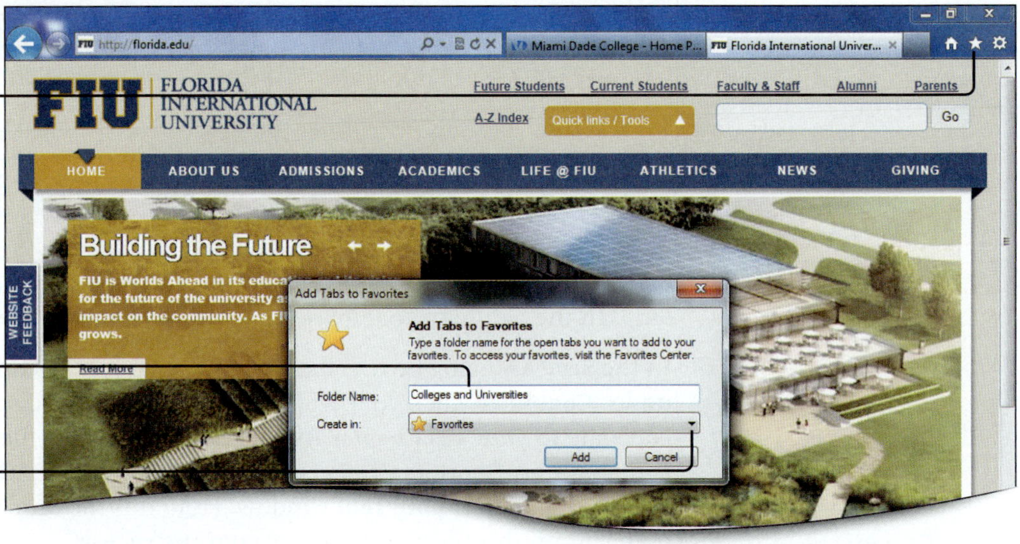

5 In the dialog box, click the **Add** button. **Close** Internet Explorer and all tabs.

6 Open **Internet Explorer** again, and then in the upper right corner, click the **View favorites, feeds, and history** button. If necessary, at the top of the displayed list, click the Favorites tab. Scroll down if necessary, and then point to the arrow to the right of **Colleges and Universities** to display the ScreenTip. Compare your screen with Figure 1.23.

Figure 1.23

7 To the right of **Colleges and Universities**, click the arrow to open the entire group of sites on individual tabs. Point to the tab for your home page, right-click, and then click **Close tab** so that only the two Florida college tabs display. Notice that because they are in a group, the tabs are colored to match.

From the Favorites list, you can also open the folder and click one of the links individually to open just one of the sites.

8 Display the tab for **Florida International University**, and then on the navigation bar on the left of this site, click **Colleges and Schools**. Locate and click the link for the **College of Business Administration**.

9 Click the **View favorites, feeds, and history** button, click **Add to favorites**, and then in the **Add a Favorite** dialog box, click the **Create in arrow**. Compare your screen with Figure 1.24.

Figure 1.24

10 From the displayed list, click the **Colleges and Universities** folder, and then click the **Add** button.

The link to the College of Business Administration at Florida International University is added to the folder *Colleges and Universities*.

11 Open a **New Tab**, type **miamidade.gov** and then press Enter.

12 Press Ctrl + D—this is a keyboard shortcut for the Add to Favorites command. In the **Add a Favorite** dialog box, click the **New folder** button.

13 In the **Folder Name** box, type **County Govt Miami-Dade** Click the **Create in arrow**, and then click **Favorites** so that you create the folder at the same level as the other folders. Click the **Create** button.

14 In the displayed **Add a Favorite** dialog box, select the text in the **Name** box, and then replace it by typing **Miami-Dade County** Compare your screen with Figure 1.25.

You need not accept the default name of a Web site stored in your Favorites list. Change the name as necessary so that you can easily identify the site.

Figure 1.25

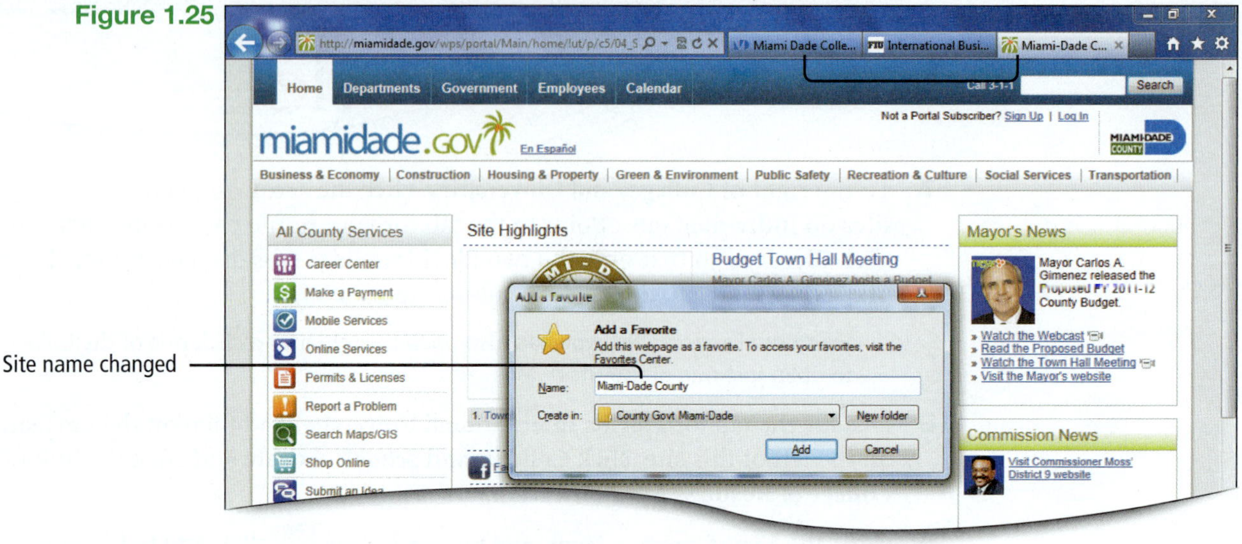

15 In the **Add a Favorite** dialog box, click the **Add** button.

In this manner, you can create folders for your favorite sites at the time you save the site as a Favorite. Be sure to notice where the folder is being stored, and place it either at the Favorites level or within other folders if you want to do so.

16 In the upper right corner, click the **View favorites, feeds, and history** button. To the right of *Add to favorites* click the arrow, click **Organize favorites**, and then in this dialog box, create a **New Folder** named **Florida Tourism** Press Enter, and then in the lower right corner of the dialog box, click the **Close** button.

17 Open a **New Tab**, type **visitflorida.com** and then press Enter. Click the **View favorites, feeds, and history** button, and then click **Add to favorites**. In the displayed dialog box, click the **Create in arrow**, click the **Florida Tourism** folder, and then **Add** this site.

18 Hold down Alt and press Z to display the **Add to favorites** menu. Click **Organize favorites**, click the **County Govt Miami-Dade** folder to select it, and then in the lower portion of the dialog box, click **Rename**. Type **Florida Government** and then press Enter.

19 Point to **Colleges and Universities** and click one time to expand the list. Click **Colleges and Universities** again to collapse the list. Point to **Florida Tourism**, and then right-click.

From the displayed shortcut menu, you can see that you can take many additional actions on the list of folders such as sorting the list of folders by name, creating a new folder, and deleting a folder.

20 Click **Colleges and Universities** to expand the list. Then point to **Florida International University** and right-click.

From the displayed menu, you can perform similar commands related to a specific site in the list.

21 **Close** [X] the **Organize Favorites** dialog box; **Close** [X] Internet Explorer.

More Knowledge | Copying Favorites from One Computer to Another and Printing Favorites

You can save your Favorites from one computer and then import that list to another computer. To do so, open Windows Help and Support, type *export Favorites*, and follow the instructions for exporting, importing, and printing favorites.

Activity 1.05 | Using the Favorites Bar

The ***Favorites bar*** is a toolbar that displays directly below the address bar and to which you can add or drag Web addresses you use frequently. You can also use the Favorites bar to monitor either RSS feeds or a ***Web Slice*** to which you have subscribed. A Web Slice is a specific portion—a slice—of a Web page to which you can subscribe, and which enables you to see when updated content, such as the current temperature, is available from a site.

1 On the taskbar, click the **Internet Explorer** button. Click in the **address bar** to select the existing URL, type **weather.gov** and then press Enter. In an open area above the **address bar**, right-click, and then on the shortcut menu, click **Favorites bar**.

The Favorites bar displays directly below the address bar. By default, the Favorites bar is turned off; however, after you turn it on, it will display every time you start Internet Explorer until you turn it off again.

2 At the left end of the **Favorites bar**, click the **Add to Favorites bar** button, and then compare your screen with Figure 1.26.

Figure 1.26

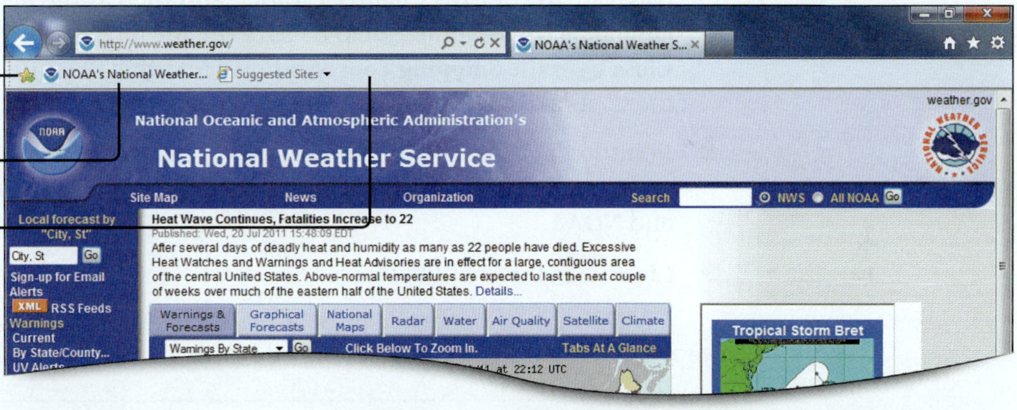

3 Click in the **address bar**, type **fsu.edu** and press Enter. At the left end of the **address bar**, point to the **Florida State University logo**, hold down the left mouse button, and then drag the logo onto the **Favorites bar** until a black line displays to the right of NOAA's site, as shown in Figure 1.27. Then release the mouse button.

Figure 1.27

4 On the **Favorites bar**, point to the NOAA site, right-click, and then click **Rename**. In the **Rename** box, type **NOAA** and then click **OK**. Using the same technique, rename *The Florida State University* link **FSU** and then compare your screen with Figure 1.28.

You can change and shorten the names on your Favorites bar to make additional space. When you have more Favorites than the bar can accommodate, arrows will display at the right, which when clicked will display a continuation of the list.

Figure 1.28

5 Click in the **address bar**, type **ufl.edu** and press Enter, and then drag its logo to the **Favorites bar** to the right of FSU.

6 **Start** the **Snipping Tool** program, click the **New arrow**, and then click **Full-screen Snip**. In the **Snipping Tool** mark-up window, click the **Save Snip** button.

7 In the **Save As** dialog box, in the **navigation pane**, scroll down as necessary, and then under **Computer**, click your USB flash drive so that it displays in the **address bar**. Navigate to your **IE9 Chapter 1** folder, and then as the file name, type **Lastname_Firstname_1A_Favorites_Snip** Be sure the file type is **JPEG file**, and then press Enter. **Close** the **Snipping Tool** window. Hold this file until you finish Project 1A, and then submit this file as directed by your instructor.

8 Point to the **University of Florida** link on the **Favorites bar**, right-click, click **Delete**, and then if necessary click **Yes**. By using the same technique, delete the links for **FSU** and **NOAA**.

9 **Close** Internet Explorer.

On your own computer, place links to the sites you use most frequently on the Favorites bar, and for other favorite sites, add them to the Favorites Center.

More Knowledge | Additional Tools to Manage Your Favorites

There are additional free tools available to manage your favorites. These tools are sometimes referred to as ***bookmark managers***. Windows Live Favorites (*http://favorites.live.com*) is a free Web-based service from Microsoft. The Favorites you place on this list are available from *any* online connection—not just from your own computer. (Note: You will need to sign up for a Windows Live account, which is also free.)

Objective 3 | Manage Browsing History and Browse with InPrivate

As you browse the Web, Internet Explorer stores information about the Web sites you visit. It also stores information that you are frequently asked to provide. For example, if you type your name and address into a Web site, Internet Explorer stores that information. All of this information is referred to as your ***browsing history***.

Usually it is useful to have this information stored on your computer, because it speeds your Web browsing and might automatically provide information so that you do not have to type it over and over.

Internet Explorer stores the following types of information:

- ***Temporary Internet files***, which are copies of Web pages, images, and media that you have downloaded from the Web. Storing this information makes viewing faster the next time you visit a site that you have visited before.
- ***Cookies***, which are small text files that Web sites put on your computer to store information about you and your preferences, for example login information.
- A history of Web sites that you have visited.
- Information that you have entered into Web sites or the address bar, including your name and address if you have entered it into a site, and the URLs that you have visited before.
- Saved Web user names and passwords.

Activity 1.06 | Viewing and Deleting Browsing History

You might want to delete your browsing history to make more space on your own computer. If you are using a public computer, such as in your college classroom or lab, you will want to delete your browsing history so that you do not leave any of your personal information stored there.

1 On the taskbar, click the **Internet Explorer** button. In the address bar, type **usa.gov** Click the **View favorites, feeds, and history** button, and then at the top of the pane click the **History tab**. Under **History**, click the **arrow**, and then if necessary, click **View By Date**. Click **Today**, and then compare your screen with Figure 1.29.

Here you can view a list of the sites you visited today.

Figure 1.29

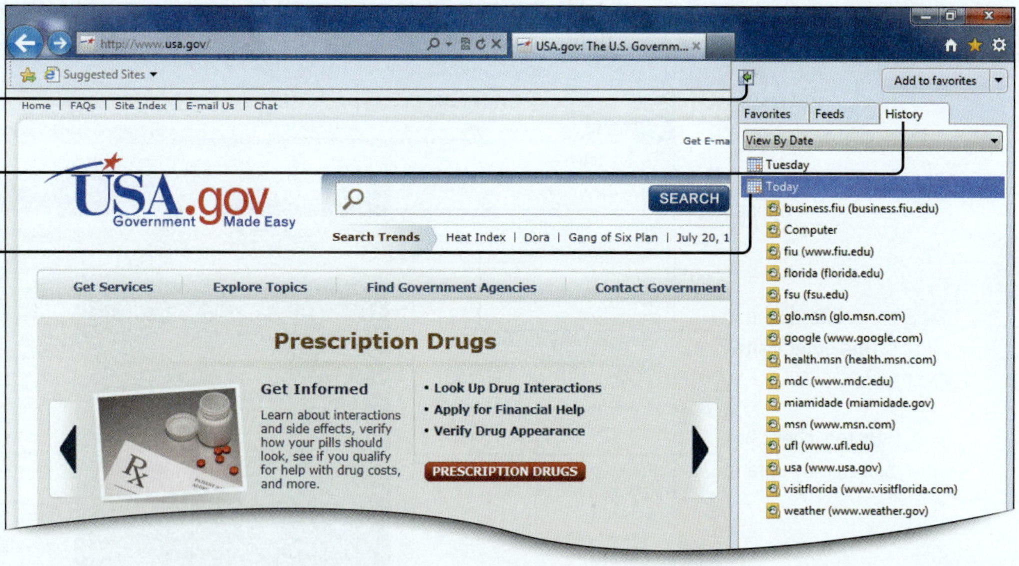

2 At the top of the pane, click the **Pin the Favorites Center** button. In the **address bar**, type **pearsonhighered.com** press Enter, and then notice that the URL has been added to the **Today** list of visited sites. Compare your screen with Figure 1.30.

Figure 1.30

Favorites Center pane pinned to side of window

Pearson site added to History list

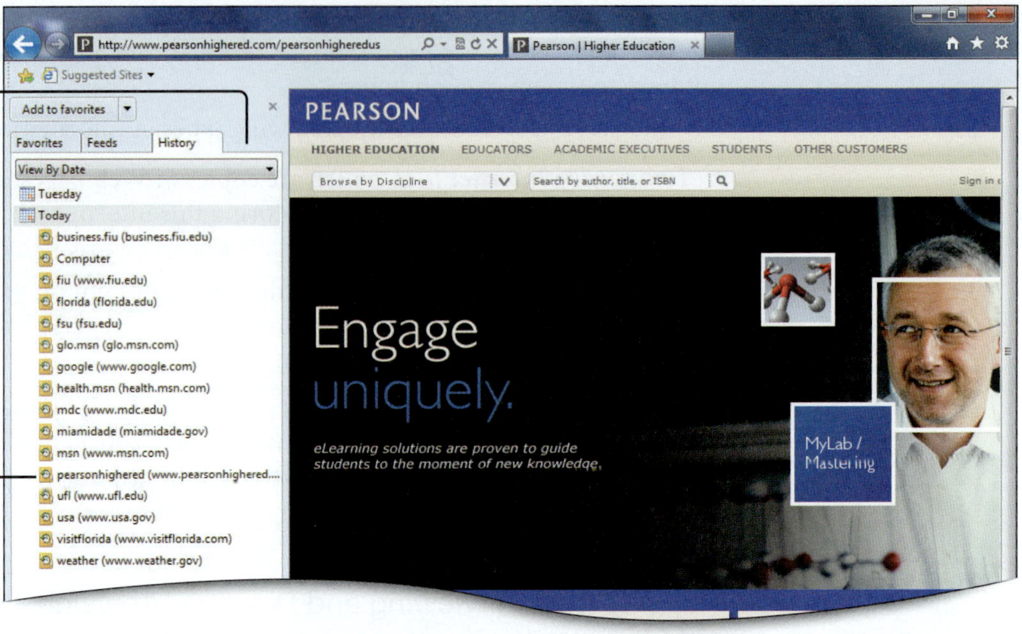

3 At the top of the pane, to the right of *View By Date*, click the **arrow**. On the displayed list, click **Search History**, and then in the displayed **Search for** box, type **Miami** Click the **Search now** button, and then notice that a list of sites that you have visited related to *Miami* displays.

4 To the right of *Search History*, click the **arrow** again, and then click **View By Order Visited Today**.

5 In an open area above the **address bar**, right-click, and then on the shortcut menu, click **Command bar**. On the **Command bar**, click the **Safety** button, and then click **Delete browsing history**. Compare your screen with Figure 1.31.

The ***Command bar*** contains, by default, the buttons to view your Home page settings; view your Feeds; view mail; print Web pages; manipulate Web pages, for example by saving; select Safety settings; display a list of Tools; and get Help.

Figure 1.31

Command bar opened

Sites listed in the order visited

History check box selected by default

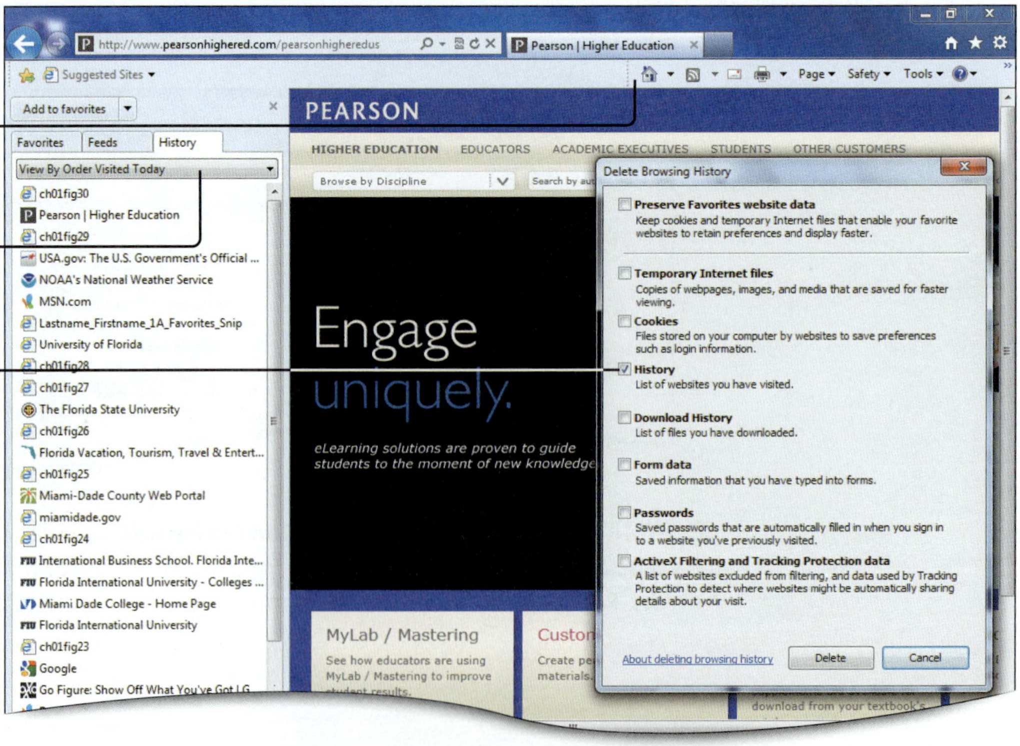

6 Clear all but the **History** check box. Unless you are working on your own computer and you do not want to delete any files, click the **Delete** button, and then wait a few moments for the deletion to complete.

Deleting all browsing history does not delete your list of Favorites or feeds to which you have subscribed. This action deletes only temporary files, your browsing history, cookies, and saved form information passwords—if their checkboxes are selected.

If you perform this action on your own computer, it might take a few seconds longer to display sites again the first time you access them. After that, the system will rebuild your browsing history as you browse the Web.

7 **Close** the Favorites Center, and then **Close** Internet Explorer.

More Knowledge | Close Internet Explorer After Deleting Browser History

You should close Internet Explorer after deleting your browser history to clear cookies that are still in memory from your current browsing session. This is especially important when using a public computer such as in your college computer lab.

Activity 1.07 | Using InPrivate Browsing

Use ***InPrivate Browsing*** to browse the Web without storing data about your browsing session. This feature is useful because it prevents anyone else who might be using your computer from seeing what sites you visited.

1 On the taskbar, click the **Internet Explorer** button. Click the **New Tab** button. On the **Command bar**, click the **Safety arrow**, and then click **InPrivate Browsing**. Compare your screen with Figure 1.32.

The InPrivate indicator displays on the address bar and the tab indicates *InPrivate.*

Figure 1.32

InPrivate browsing is turned on

Safety button arrow

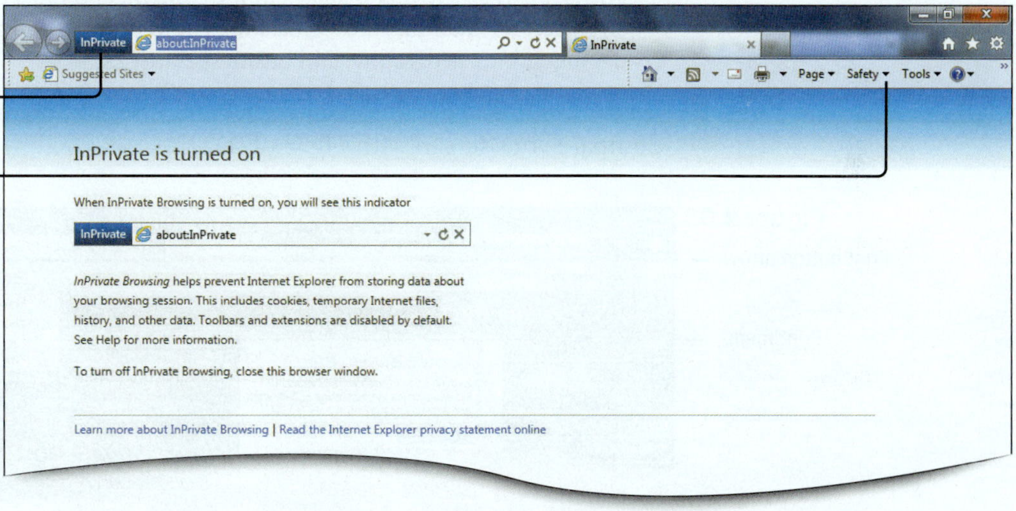

2 With the text in the **address bar** selected, type **gatorzone.com** and press Enter. (This site may play sound if your speakers or headphones are enabled.)

3 Click the **New Tab** button; and notice that **InPrivate Browsing** is still in effect. Type **fsu.edu/athletics** and press Enter.

In the current Internet Explorer window, you can open as many tabs as you want, and they will be protected by InPrivate Browsing.

4 Click the **View favorites, feeds, and history** button, and then click the **History tab**. Notice that the two sites you accessed while using InPrivate Browsing do *not* display on the list.

While using InPrivate Browsing, Internet Explorer stores some information. For example, cookies are kept in memory so pages work properly, but are cleared when you close the browser window. Temporary Internet files are also stored so pages work properly, but are deleted when you close the browser window. Web page history, form data, and passwords are not stored at all.

5 **Close** Internet Explorer.

Cookies are cleared and temporary Internet files are discarded.

Objective 4 | Print, Zoom, and Change the Text Size of Web Pages

By default, Internet Explorer 9 will shrink a Web page's text just enough to ensure that the entire page prints properly. The Page Zoom feature enables you to increase or decrease the page size for easier viewing. You can also adjust the size of displayed text.

Activity 1.08 | Printing Web Pages

Internet Explorer 9 provides useful options for formatting and then printing a Web page. In the following activity, you will work with Barbara and Steven to print a Web page.

1 **Close** any open windows. On the taskbar, click the **Internet Explorer** button, click in the **address bar**, type **census.gov** and then press Enter.

The home page that serves as the official ***portal*** for the US Census Bureau displays. A portal is a Web site that displays news, content, and links that are of interest to a specific audience; for example, individuals who need information about population statistics, demographics, geography, and business statistics.

2 On the **Command bar**, locate and click the **Print button arrow** to display a menu. Compare your screen with Figure 1.33.

Figure 1.33

Print button arrow

Print menu

3 On the menu, click **Print preview**. Compare your screen with Figure 1.34, and then take a moment to study the parts of the Print Preview window described in the table in Figure 1.35.

Recall that Internet Explorer will shrink the page as necessary to fit horizontally on the selected paper size. You can also drag the margins by using the Adjust margin buttons on this Print Preview screen.

Figure 1.34

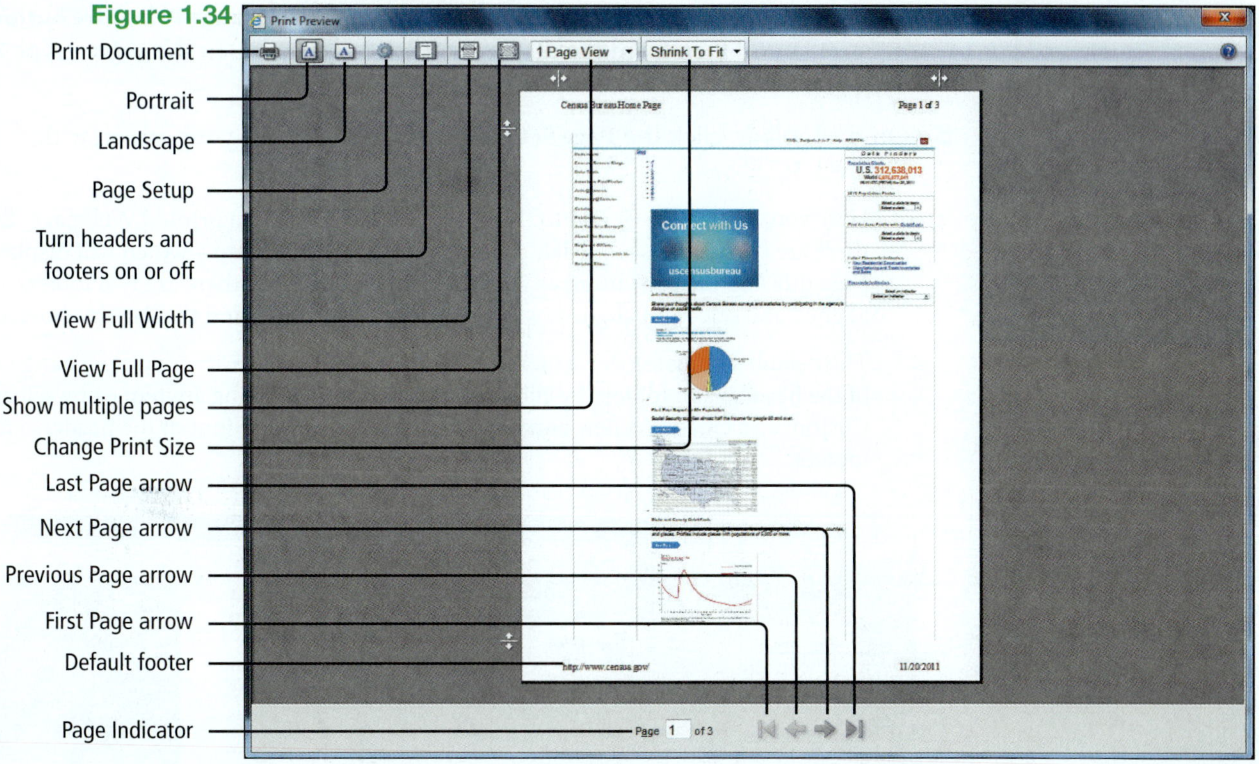

Parts of the Print Preview Window in Internet Explorer 9

Adjust margin buttons	Adjusts the left, right, top, and bottom margins by dragging.
Change Print Size	Stretches or shrinks the page size to fill the printed page.
First Page arrow	Displays the first page of a multiple-page preview screen.
Landscape	Prints the page in landscape orientation, in which the paper is wider than it is tall.
Last Page arrow	Displays the last page of a multiple-page preview screen.
Next Page arrow	Displays the next page of a multiple-page preview screen.
Page Indicator	Indicates the page displayed and the total number of pages.
Page Setup	Opens the Page Setup dialog box, in which you can change paper size, orientation, margins, and header and footer options.
Portrait	Prints the page in portrait orientation, in which the paper is taller than it is wide.
Previous Page arrow	Displays the previous page of a multiple-page preview screen.
Print Document	Opens the Print dialog box, enabling you to print the page using the current settings.
Show multiple pages	Displays multiple pages on the preview screen.
Turn headers or footers on or off	Turns the display of headers and footers off or on in the manner of a toggle button.
View Full Page	Zooms the Web page to show the full Web page in the preview screen.
View Full Width	Zooms the Web page to the width of the preview screen.

Figure 1.35

> **Another Way**
>
> Experiment with percentages on the list, or by typing in the Custom box, to shrink the page to print the way you want it to—on one or more pages.

4 On the toolbar, to the right of *Shrink To Fit*, click the **Change Print Size button arrow** [Shrink To Fit ▾], and then from the displayed list, click **Custom**. In the **% box**, type **75** and then press Enter.

5 On the toolbar, click the **Page Setup** button. Compare your screen with Figure 1.36.

Here you can change or add to the headers and footers on a printed Web page. By default there are two headers—one left aligned and one right aligned—which will display the page title and the page number with total pages. Similarly, there are two footers, one left aligned and one right aligned, which will display the URL and the date in short format.

The default setting for the centered header and footer is *Empty*. You can change any of the headers and footers by clicking the arrow and selecting an item or by selecting Custom and creating a new entry. You can also change the font of the headers and footers.

Figure 1.36

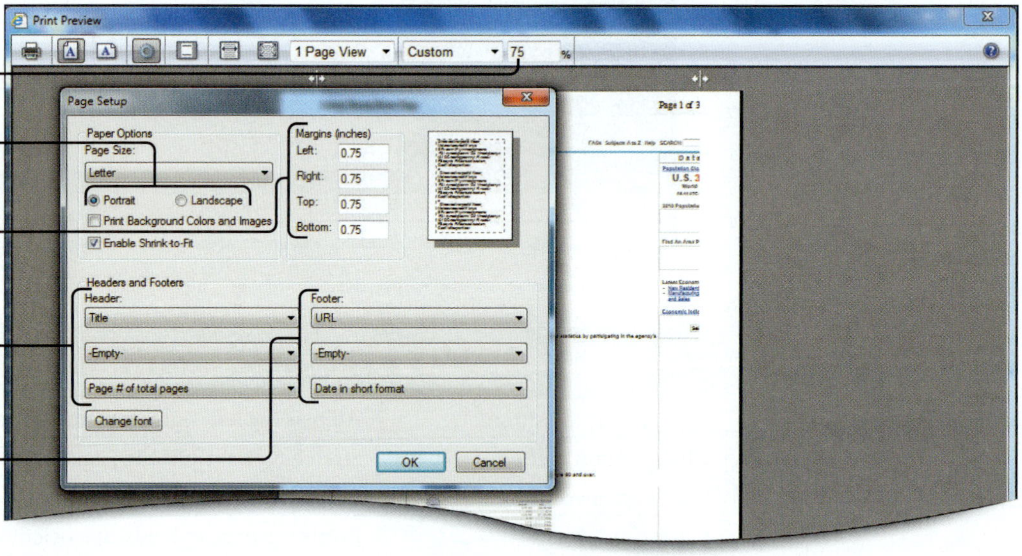

6 Under **Footer**, click the second arrow, and then click **Custom**.

Here you can enter a centered footer.

7 In the **Custom** dialog box, using your own name, type **Firstname Lastname** Compare your screen with Figure 1.37.

Figure 1.37

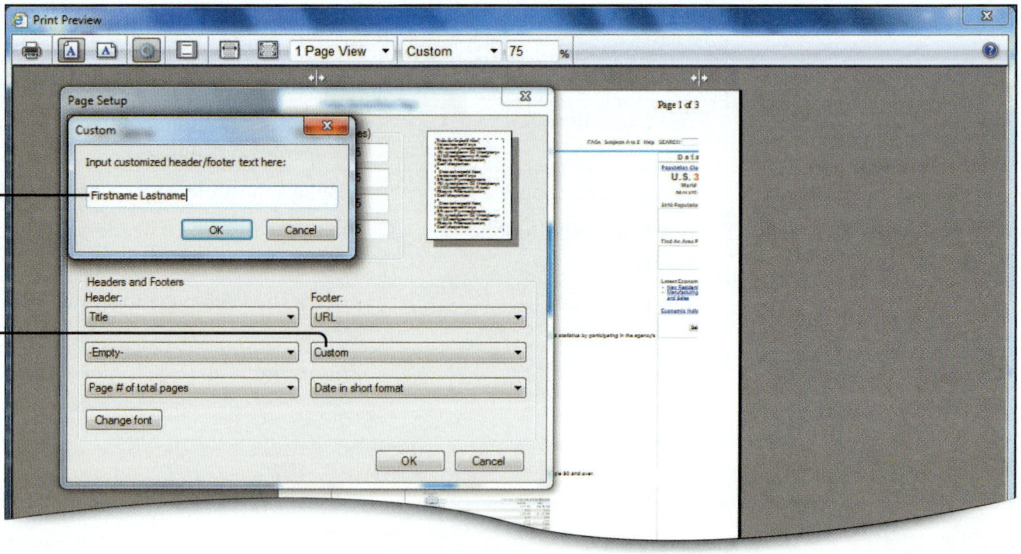

8 In the **Custom** dialog box, click **OK**. In the **Page Setup** dialog box, click **OK**.

In the Print Preview screen, your name displays as a centered footer.

9 **Start** the **Snipping Tool** program, click the **New arrow**, and then click **Window Snip**. Click anywhere in the **Print Preview** window. In the **Snipping Tool** window, click the **Save Snip** button. (Note: Your taskbar must be displayed—not hidden—to access the Snipping Tool.)

10 In the **Save As** dialog box, in the navigation pane, scroll down as necessary, and then under **Computer**, click your USB flash drive so that it displays in the **address bar**. Navigate to your **IE9 Chapter 1** folder, and then as the file name, type **Lastname_Firstname_1A_Print_Snip** Be sure the file type is **JPEG file**, and then press Enter. **Close** the **Snipping Tool** window. Hold this file until you finish Project 1A, and then submit this file as directed by your instructor.

11 **Close** the **Print Preview** screen, and then **Close** Internet Explorer.

More Knowledge | Printing Specific Parts of a Web Page

To print only a specific part of a Web page, use your mouse to select the content that you want to print. Then, click the Print button arrow, click Print, and then in the Print dialog box, click the Selection option button. Click Print.

Activity 1.09 | Zooming and Changing Web Page Text Size

1 **Close** any open windows. On the taskbar, click the **Internet Explorer** button, click in the **address bar**, type **weather.gov** and press Enter. On the **Command bar**, click the **Page** button, point to *Zoom*, and then click **200%**.

The view of the page is increased to 200%. Increasing the Zoom level increases the size of everything on the page, including graphics and controls.

2 Using the technique you just practiced, change the Zoom level to **50%**.

3 Hold down Ctrl and then turn your mouse wheel backward and forward to increase and decrease the zoom.

This is a useful technique if you want to briefly magnify some text that is difficult to read or to examine a photo closely.

4 In the lower right corner of your screen, point to the **Change zoom level button**, and then click as many times as necessary to return the zoom level to **100%**.

5 Open a **New Tab**, type **noaa.org** and then press Enter. On the **Command bar**, click the **Page** button, and then point to **Text size**.

The default text size is Medium, but if you would like to see more text on the screen you can set a smaller text size. If you have difficulty reading Web pages on your screen, you can set a larger text size.

Changing the text size affects only the text—graphics and controls continue to display in their original size.

6 On the displayed submenu, click **Largest**, and notice that the text on your screen is enlarged. Compare your screen with Figure 1.38.

Figure 1.38

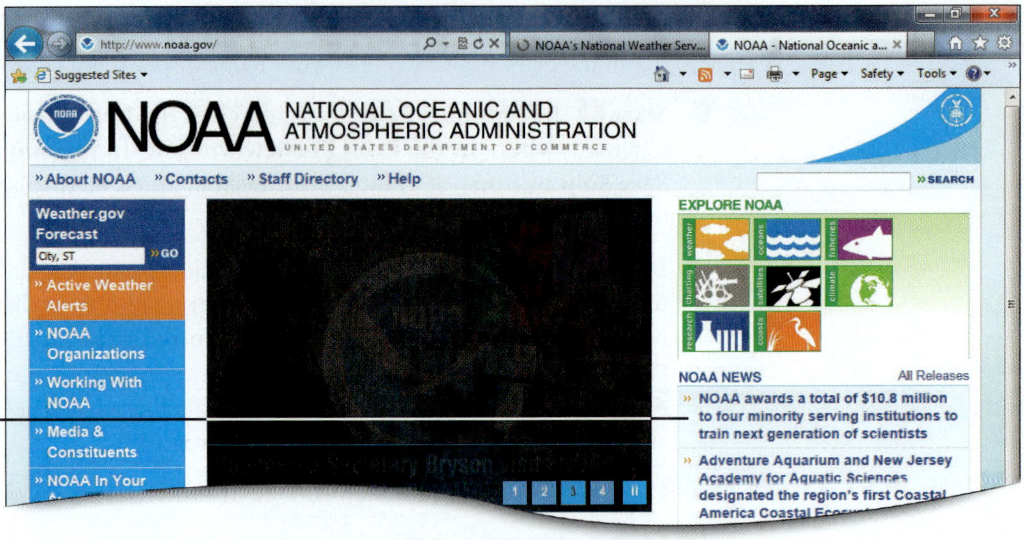

Note | Text Size is Set at Page Creation

The text size of some Web pages is set by the person who created the page. The creator of the Web page may set a specific text size that you cannot change with the *Text size* command. If you want to do so, you can override this setting as follows: Click the Tools button on the Command bar, click Internet options, on the General tab, click the Accessibility button, and then select the *Ignore font sizes specified on webpages* check box.

7 **Close** Internet Explorer.

More Knowledge | Using Full Screen Mode

You can view a Web page in Full Screen mode, which will hide the title bar, the address bar, the Favorites Bar, the tab row, and the Command bar—unless you point to them. Full Screen mode will give you another inch or so of vertical screen space. To view Full Screen mode, press F11; or, from the Tools menu, click Full Screen. Press F11 again to return to Normal view.

Objective 5 | Save Web Page Information

You can save an entire Web page, an image on a Web page, or selected text from a Web page. Doing so is a good way to capture information to which you want to refer later without accessing the Internet.

Activity 1.10 | Saving Web Page Information

1 **Close** any open windows. On the taskbar, click the **Internet Explorer** button, click in the **address bar**, type **nps.gov** and then press Enter. Compare your screen with Figure 1.39. If you cannot locate this page, navigate to any page that has a picture or graphic.

Because the content of Web pages changes frequently, the content and images on the displayed page will likely differ from Figure 1.39.

Figure 1.39

US National Park Service (your text and images will differ)

Image on the page

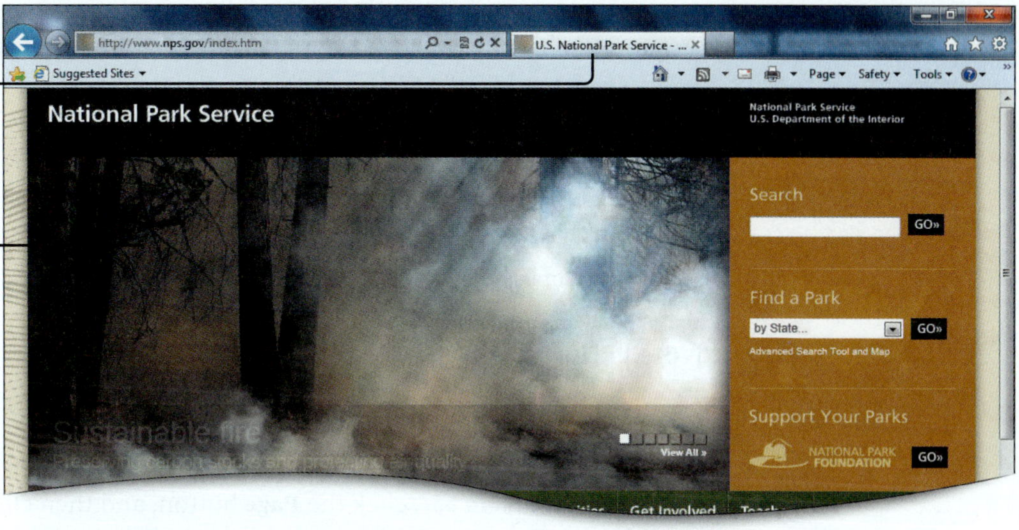

> **Alert! | The Content of Web Pages is Protected by Copyright Laws**
>
> Nearly everything you find on the Web is protected by copyright law, which protects authors of original works, including text, art, photographs, and music. If you want to use text or images that you find online, you will need to get permission. One of the exceptions to this law is the use of small amounts of information for educational purposes, which falls under Fair Use guidelines. Copyright laws in the United States are open to different interpretations, and copyright laws can be very different in other countries. As a general rule, if you want to use someone else's material, always get permission first.

2 Point to any picture or image on the page (scroll down if necessary to find a picture, or navigate to some other page with a picture), right-click, and then from the displayed menu, click **Save picture as**. If necessary, navigate to the **Pictures** library in your personal folder, and then in the **File name** box, type **Yosemite_Fire** Compare your screen with Figure 1.40.

You can save a picture displayed on a Web page in this manner.

Figure 1.40

Save Picture dialog box

Pictures library active

File name typed

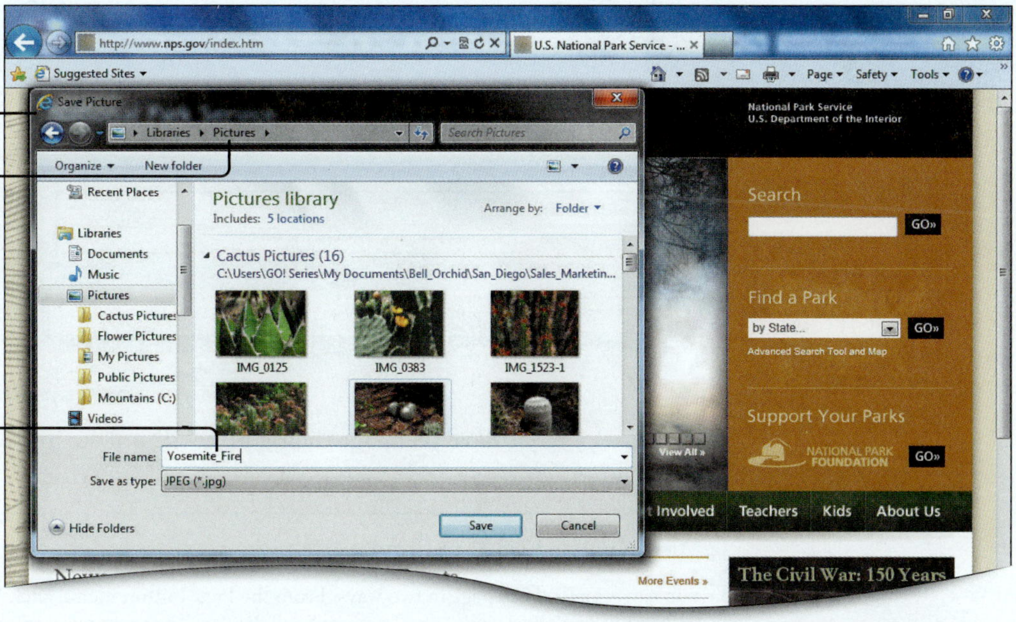

3 With the **Save Picture** dialog box displayed, **Start** the **Snipping Tool** program, click the **New arrow**, and then click **Full-screen Snip**. In the **Snipping Tool** window, click the **Save Snip** button.

4 In the **Save As** dialog box, in the **navigation pane**, scroll down as necessary, and then under **Computer**, click your USB flash drive so that it displays in the **address bar**. Navigate to your **IE9 Chapter 1** folder, and then as the file name, type **Lastname_Firstname_1A_Picture_Snip** Be sure the file type is **JPEG file**, and then press Enter. **Close** the **Snipping Tool** window. Hold this file until you finish Project 1A, and then submit this file as directed by your instructor.

5 In the **Save Picture** dialog box, click **Cancel**.

You can use this technique to save images on Web pages.

> **Note | Printing a Picture from a Web Page**
>
> To print a picture from a Web page, point to the image and right-click. From the displayed menu, click Print picture, and then in the Print dialog box, click Print.

6 On the **Command bar**, click the **Page** button, and then click **Save as**. At the bottom of the displayed **Save Webpage** dialog box, click the **Save as type arrow**, and then compare your screen with Figure 1.41.

To save all files associated with the page, including graphics, frames, and style sheets in their original format, you can use the file format *Webpage, complete (*.htm;*.html)*.

To save all information as a single file, you can use the file format *Web Archive, single file (*.mht)*.

To save just the current HTML page, without graphics, sounds, or other files, you can use the file format *Webpage, HTML only (*.htm;*.html)*. To save just the text from the current Web page, you can use the file format *Text File (*.txt)*.

Figure 1.41

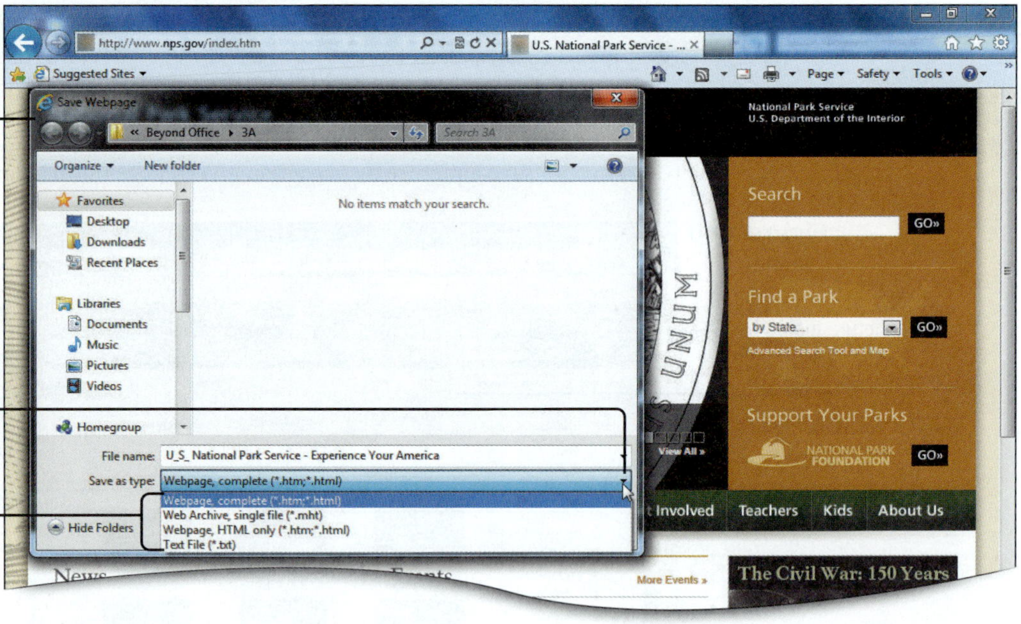

7 **Close** the **Save Webpage** dialog box without saving, and then **Close** Internet Explorer.

> **More Knowledge | E-mailing a Web Page**
>
> You can e-mail a Web page in two ways. From the Page button menu, click *Send page by e-mail*; or, click *Send link by e-mail*. Your default e-mail program will display. The first option inserts the entire page in the text of the e-mail. The second option inserts only the URL in the text of the e-mail message.
>
> To set a program to use for e-mail within Internet Explorer, on the Command bar, click the Tools button, click Internet options, click the Programs tab, and then under Internet programs, click the Set programs button.

Objective 6 | Manage Add-ons

An ***add-on*** is a program that adds features to a Web browser such as Internet Explorer. Examples of add-ons include additional toolbars, animated mouse pointers, and interactive Web content. Most add-ons come from the Internet and most require that you give permission to install them on your computer. It is possible that an add-on is installed without your knowledge, for example as part of another program. Some add-ons are installed with Microsoft Windows 7.

Activity 1.11 | Managing Add-ons

1 **Close** any open windows. On the taskbar, click the **Internet Explorer** button. A Notification bar may display at the bottom of your screen. If it does, click the **Choose add-ons** button, and then compare your screen with Figure 1.42.

A ***Notification bar*** displays information about pending downloads, security issues, add-ons, and other related issues that might be important to the operation of your computer. The *add-ons* notification displays occasionally when you open Internet Explorer. You can choose to disable some of the add-ons, leave them running, or ignore the message and close the Notification bar.

Figure 1.42

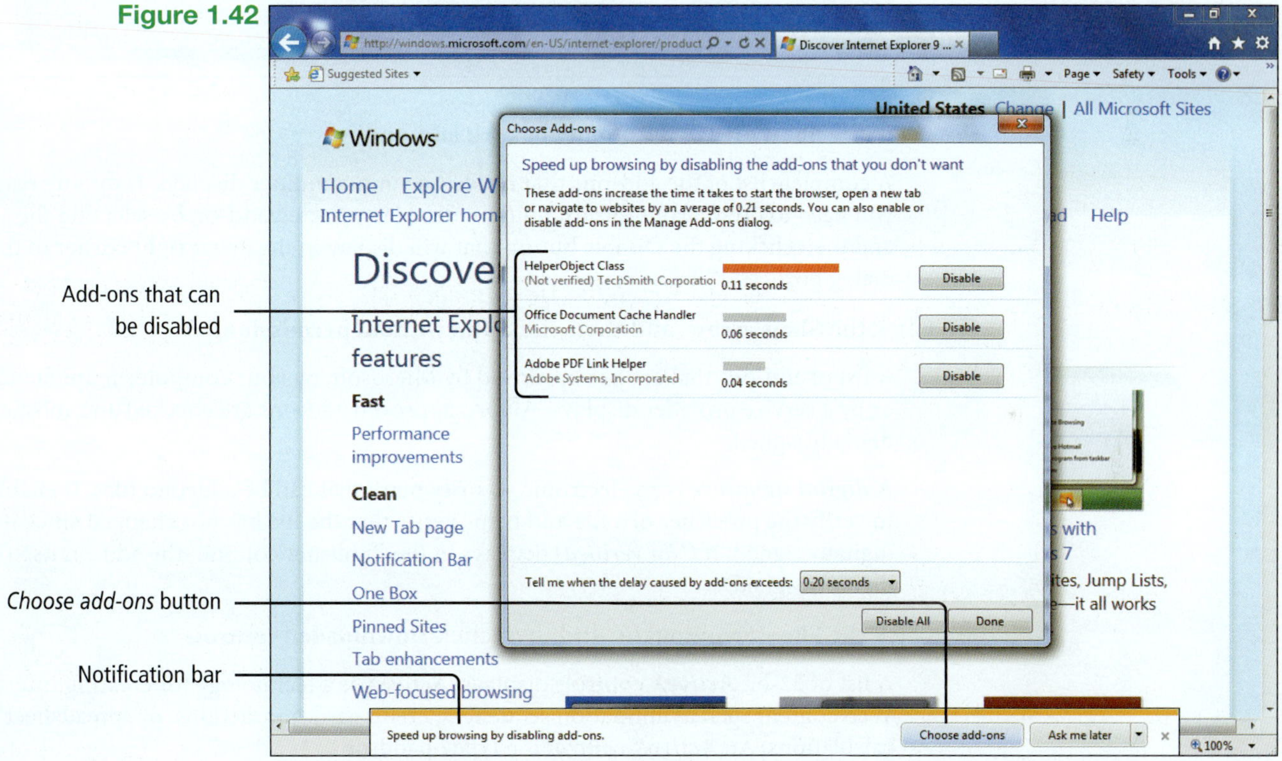

2 If you displayed this screen, in the **Choose Add-ons** dialog box, click **Done** to close both the dialog box and the Notification bar.

3 Click in the **address bar**, type **florida.edu** and then press Enter. On the **Command bar**, click the **Tools** button, and then click **Manage add-ons**. Compare your screen with Figure 1.43. Be sure that **Show** indicates *Currently loaded add-ons*.

The add-ons that are necessary for the current Web page or a recently viewed Web page display on this list. This dialog box gives you far more control over add-ons than the dialog box opened from the Notification bar.

Figure 1.43

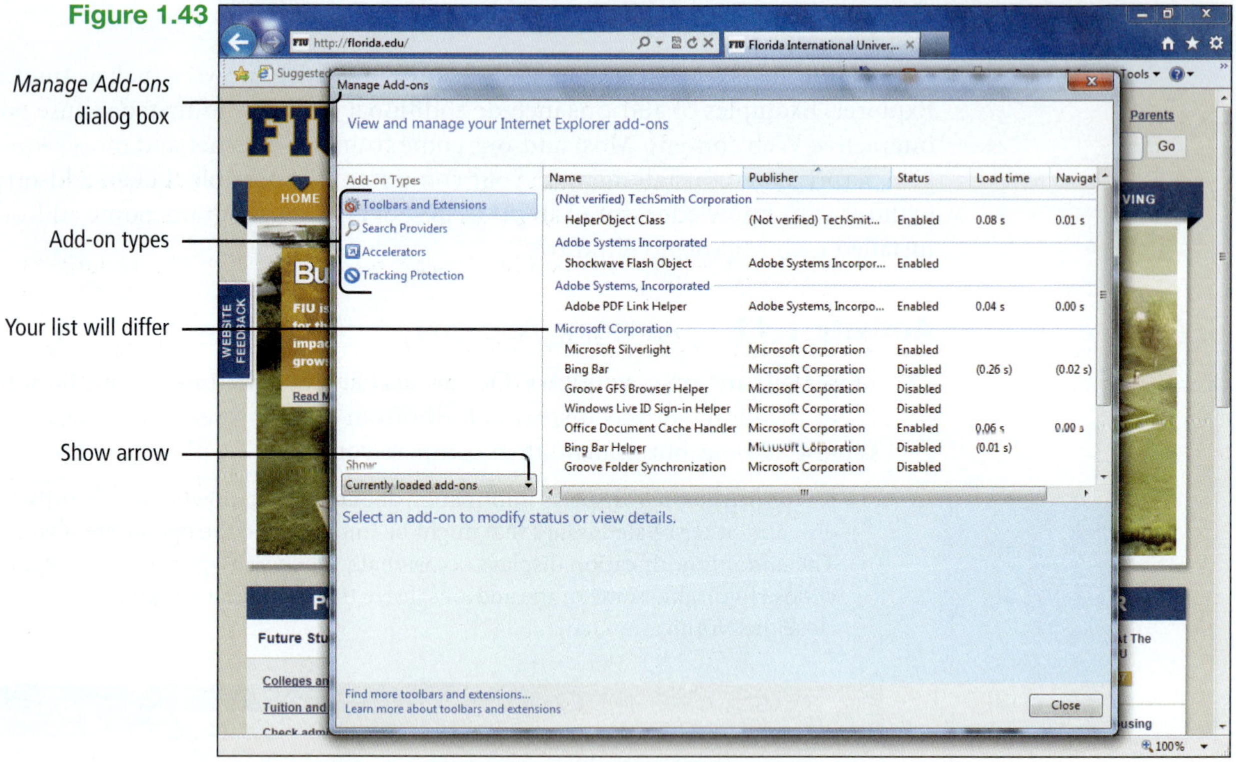

4 Click the **Show arrow**, and then click **All add-ons**.

A complete list of the add-ons that reside on your computer displays. If for any reason you need to do so, from this list you can disable a selected add-on by selecting the add-on, and then clicking the Disable button that will display in the lower right corner of the dialog box.

5 Click the **Show arrow**, and then click **Run without permission**.

A list of add-ons that are pre-approved by Microsoft, by your computer manufacturer, or by a service provider displays. All pre-approved add-ons are checked and most are digitally signed.

A ***digital signature*** is an electronic security mark that can be added to files. It enables you to verify the publisher of a file and helps verify that the file has not changed since it was digitally signed. If *(Not verified)* displays in the Publisher column, the add-on itself is not digitally signed.

6 Click the **Show arrow** again, and then click **Downloaded controls**.

A list of 32-bit ***ActiveX*** controls displays. ActiveX is a technology for creating interactive Web content such as animation sequences, credit card transactions, or spreadsheet calculations. An ***ActiveX control*** is a type of add-on.

When displaying some Web pages, you might see a Notification bar near the bottom of the screen. A Notification bar commonly displays information about downloads, blocked pop-up windows, add-ons, and installing ActiveX controls.

Use caution when asked to download an ActiveX control. Such controls can enhance your Web browsing, but could also be a security risk. Be sure you trust the site that is asking you to install the control.

7 In the lower left corner of the **Manage Add-ons** dialog box, click the link **Find more toolbars and extensions**. In the **Command bar**, click **add-ons**.

The Microsoft site for Internet Explorer Add-ons displays.

8 Scroll to the bottom of the page and click **Get Add-ons**. Take a moment to examine this page.

You can see that there are many interesting and useful add-ons that you can add to Internet Explorer.

9 To change the text size back to the default setting, on the **Command bar**, click the **Page** button. Point to **Text size**, and then click **Medium**.

The larger text size may be easier to read, but it also reduces the amount of information displayed on the screen.

10 **Close** all open windows, and then **Close** Internet Explorer. Submit the five snip files from this project to your instructor as directed.

End **You have completed Project 1A**

Project 1B Searching with Search Tools and Using the Web Safely

Project Activities

In Activities 1.12 through 1.18 you will train with Steven Ramos and Barbara Hewitt, employees in the Information Technology Department at the Bell Orchid Hotel, so that you will be able to search the Web from the Internet Explorer window and maintain the safety and security of data and computer users. Your completed screens will look similar to Figure 1.44.

Project Files

For Project 1B, you will need the following files:

New Snip files

You will save your files as:

Lastname_Firstname_1B_Searches_Snip
Lastname_Firstname_1B_RSS_Snip
Lastname_Firstname_1B_Slices_Snip
Lastname_Firstname_1B_Accelerator_Snip

Project Results

Figure 1.44
Project 1B

Objective 7 | Search the Internet

The Internet can connect you to a vast amount of information, but first you have to find the information that you need. From within Internet Explorer, there are two ways in which you can search for information on the Internet *without* navigating to a specific Web site. The easiest method is to type a ***search term***, which is a word or phrase that describes the topic about which you want to find information, directly into the address bar. When you type a search term directly in the address bar, Internet Explorer tries to find a URL that matches; if it cannot do so, the default search provider conducts the search. You can also type a search term in a Search box if one is displayed in your Internet Explorer window.

Activity 1.12 | Searching the Internet

A ***search provider*** is a Web site that provides search capabilities on the Web. The default search provider in Internet Explorer is Microsoft's Bing; however, you can change the default and easily switch among providers.

1 On the taskbar, click the **Internet Explorer** button. If necessary, enable the Favorites bar and the Command bar by right-clicking above the address bar and selecting them from the menu. Then, on the right side of the **address bar**, click the **Show Address bar Autocomplete** button, and then compare your screen with Figure 1.45.

At the bottom of the list, the Bing button displays by default. Your computer may display the buttons for other search providers. Here, Figure 1.45 shows that the Favorites bar and the Command bar are enabled.

Figure 1.45

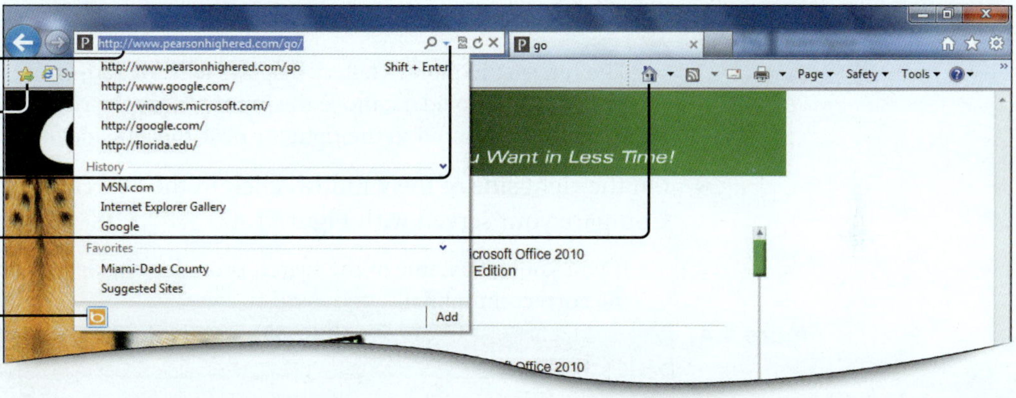

2 If you have icons for more than one search provider, click the **Bing** button. Click in the **address bar**, and then, being sure to include the quotation marks, type **"florida tourism"** and press Enter. Compare your screen with Figure 1.46. Scroll down and notice that in the list of results, your exact term *florida tourism* displays in bold.

Bing displays the search results, and above and to the right of the search results, Bing displays ***sponsored links***—paid advertisements shown as links, typically for products and services related to your search term. Sponsored links are the way that search sites like Bing, Google, and others earn revenue. On the left, related searches are suggested.

Use quotation marks to search for specific phrases. Surrounding terms with quotation marks limits the search results to only those Web pages that contain the exact phrase that you typed. Without the quotation marks, the search results will include any page that contains the terms that you typed, regardless of the order or location of the words.

Figure 1.46

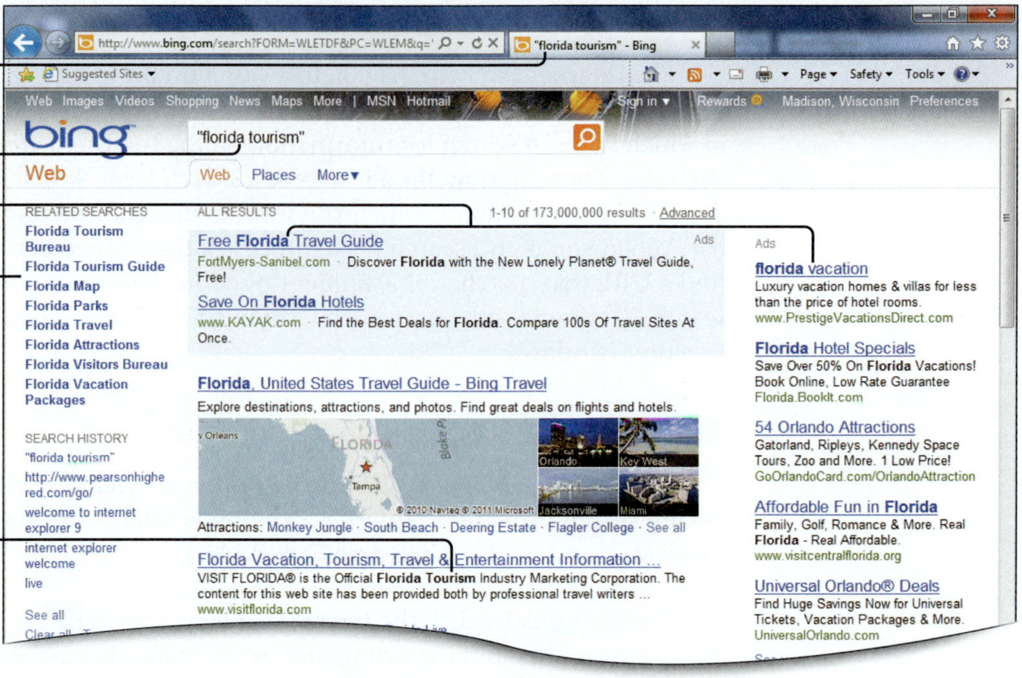

> **Note | If Bing is not your default**
>
> If Bing is not the default, set it as the default for this project as follows: On the Command bar, click the Tools button, and then click Manage add-ons. On the left, click Search Providers, and then under Name, click Bing. At the bottom of the dialog box, click the *Set as default* button, and then click the Close button to close the dialog box.

3 On the right side of the **address bar**, click the **Show Address bar Autocomplete** button [▾], and then click **Add**.

The Internet Explorer Gallery displays a list of add-ons for Internet Explorer 9. To see more search providers, move the pointer near the right side of the window over the thumbnails to scroll to the right, or near the left side of the window to scroll left.

4 On the right side of the window, click in the **Search** box, type **ask** and then press Enter. Compare your screen with Figure 1.47.

If you know the name of the search provider, the Search box is the quickest way to display the correct thumbnail.

Figure 1.47

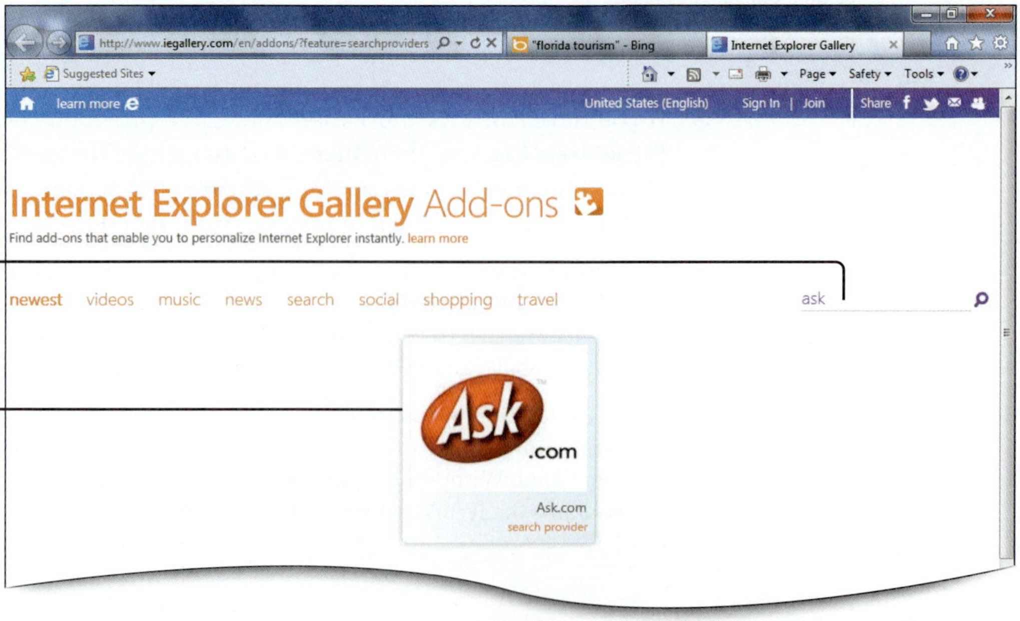

5 Click the **Ask.com** logo, and then click **Add to Internet Explorer**. If the search provider is already installed, click OK. Otherwise, in the **Add Search Provider** dialog box, click **Add**. **Close** [x] the **Internet Explorer Gallery tab**.

6 On the right side of the **address bar**, click the **Show Address bar Autocomplete** button [▾]. Notice that the Ask.com button displays in the row of search providers. Compare your screen with Figure 1.48.

Figure 1.48

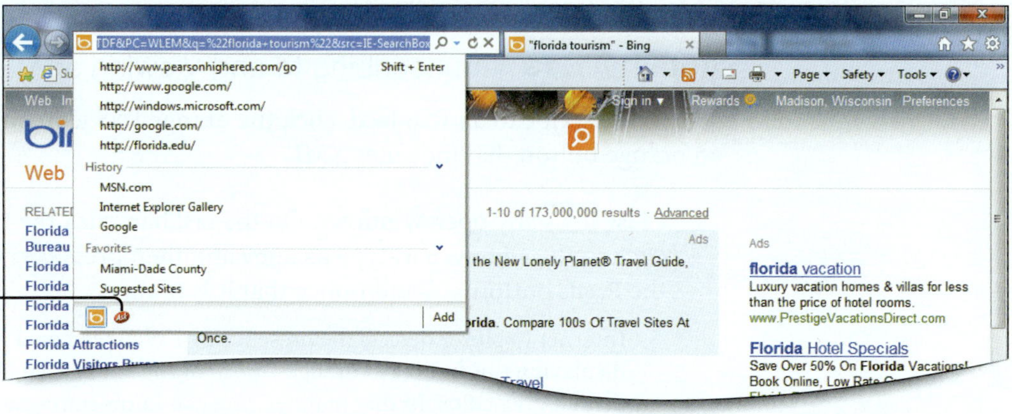

Ask.com added to list of search providers

7 On the displayed list, click the **Ask.com** button, type **"florida tourism"** and then press Enter.

Internet Explorer conducts your search for *florida tourism* in the Ask.com search engine. If you do not find what you are looking for with a particular search provider, you can search using a different provider.

8 Using the technique you used to add the Ask.com search provider, add the **Google** provider, and then **Close** [x] the **Internet Explorer Gallery tab**. Perform a **Google** search for **"florida tourism"**

Results for *florida tourism* from your Google search display.

9 **Start** the **Snipping Tool** program and create a **Full-screen Snip**. **Save** the snip in your **IE9 Chapter 1** folder as a **JPEG file** with the name **Lastname_Firstname_1B_Searches_Snip** **Close** the **Snipping Tool** window. Hold this file until you complete Project 1B, and then submit it as directed by your instructor.

10 **Close** Internet Explorer.

Objective 8 | Subscribe to and View an RSS Feed

RSS is an acronym for *Really Simple Syndication*, which is a syndication format popular for aggregating—gathering together—updates to blogs and news sites.

An ***RSS feed***—also known as an ***XML feed***, ***syndicated content***, or a ***Web feed***—contains frequently updated content published by a Web site. The feed consists of a list of new articles from a specific site, each with a headline, summary information, usually a date and time stamp, and a link to the full article for each item.

The advantage of an RSS feed is that you can view new information from your favorite Web sites instead of navigating to the site and scanning it for any new information. You do not have to constantly check a news site, for example, to see if anything new has been posted.

For example, if you regularly visit several sites daily—such as a national news site, a site related to your job, and a site with financial or stock market information—you can subscribe to an RSS feed for those sites and the new articles will be delivered to you as they become available.

Getting started with RSS involves two steps:

- Get an ***RSS viewer***: An RSS viewer, also referred to as a ***feed reader***, is a program that displays RSS feeds to which you have subscribed. There are a number of RSS viewers available, including the one that comes with Internet Explorer.
- Subscribe to feeds: Most Web sites let you know that you can syndicate their content by displaying an orange button. Clicking the button adds the feed to your feed reader list.

Activity 1.13 | Subscribing to and Viewing an RSS Feed

To subscribe to an RSS feed, click the orange RSS icon on any Web page, or look for an orange button that indicates *XML*.

1 **Close** [X] any open windows. On the taskbar, click the **Internet Explorer** button [e], click in the **address bar**, type **usa.gov** and then press Enter. On the **Command bar**, locate the **Feeds** button [RSS], and notice that it is orange.

Internet Explorer detects the presence of a Web feed on a page that you are viewing by displaying this button in orange—or in orange with a small starburst—instead of in its default gray color. In that manner, you can know immediately if feeds are available from the displayed Web page.

2 On the **Command bar**, click the **Feeds button arrow** [RSS], and then from the displayed list, click **USA.gov Updates: News and Features**. Compare your screen with Figure 1.49.

Figure 1.49

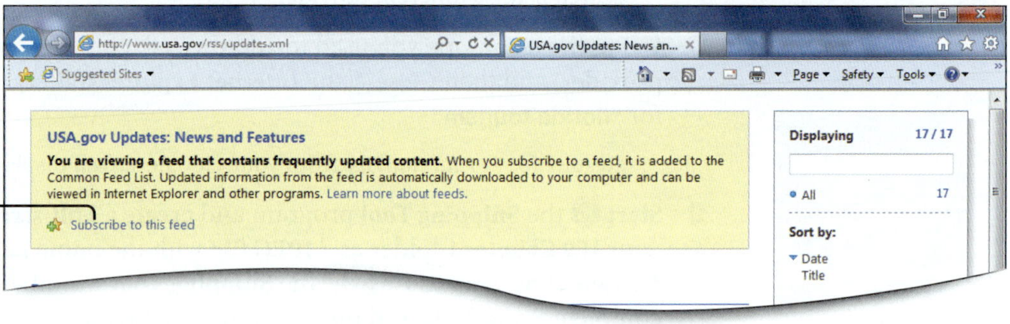

Click here to subscribe to USA.gov feed

3 In the upper left portion of the screen, click **Subscribe to this feed**. If another student has subscribed to this feed on this computer already, you will not see the *Subscribe to this feed* indication.

An Internet Explorer dialog box displays, indicating that if you subscribe, the feed will be added to your Favorites Center and kept up to date. The feed will be created in the Feeds folder.

Here, using the same techniques you use when saving a new Favorite, you can give the feed a more descriptive name, and, optionally file it in a subfolder of the Feeds folder or create a new folder.

4 In the dialog box, click the **Subscribe** button, and notice that in the upper portion of the screen, the message *You've successfully subscribed to this feed!* displays. Just below that message, click **View my feeds**. In the displayed list in the **Favorites Center**, point to the new feed name to display its ScreenTip, and then compare your screen with Figure 1.50.

When you subscribe to the feed, Internet Explorer automatically checks the Web site and downloads new content so you can see what is new since you last visited the feed.

When a new post appears, the link for that site displays in bold and clicking it shows the unread material in your browser window.

Figure 1.50

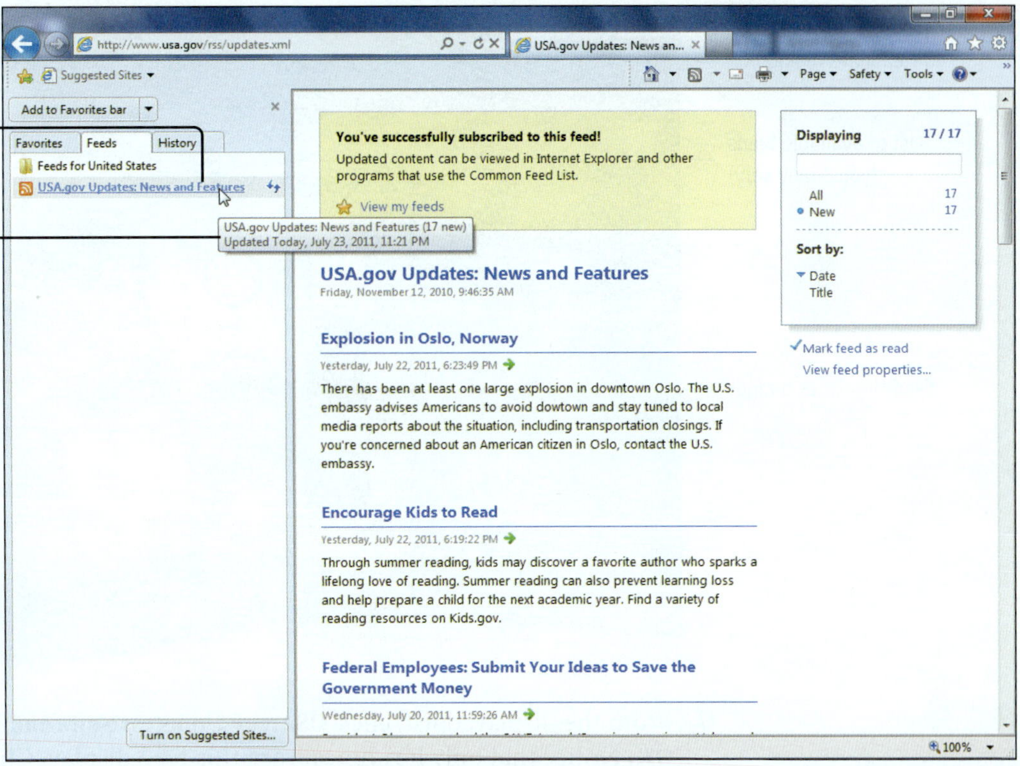

The *USA.gov* feed displays in your Favorites Center (your list may differ)

ScreenTip (yours will differ)

5 In the upper right corner of the **Favorites Center** pane, click the **Close** button.

All feeds that you open from within the Favorites Center of Internet Explorer will display in this uniform manner.

On the right, you can click various options for displaying and sorting the articles. You can also open the link to the Feed Properties dialog box, where you can adjust how often the feed is updated and the number of updates to display.

Use the *Mark feed as read* link so that if you return to this page, no current entries will be marked as new. This is useful because you do not have to remember if you have already seen an article.

6 **Close** Internet Explorer. Be sure your **Windows 7** desktop displays. Right-click on the desktop, and then click **Gadgets**. Double-click the **Feed Headlines** gadget to add it to your desktop.

Alert! | Does your screen differ?

If you are unable to display the *Feed Headlines* gadget, skip the remainder of this activity; or, just read the steps and examine the figures.

7 Wait a few moments for the gadget to load. Then, on the desktop, point to the **Feed Headlines** gadget, right-click, and click **Options**. In the displayed **Feed Headlines** dialog box, click the **Display this feed arrow**, and then compare your screen with Figure 1.51.

The feeds to which you subscribed in Internet Explorer display on the list—others might also display.

Figure 1.51

8 From the displayed list, click **USA.gov Updates: News and Features**, and then click **OK**. Notice that only headlines from this feed display. Click any headline, and then compare your screen with Figure 1.52.

To view a summary of an interesting headline, you can click any headline, as shown in Figure 1.52. In this manner, you can use a gadget to view feeds from a single source quickly. To view the entire article, click the headline in the title bar above the summary to open the Web page that contains the entire article, or click *Read online*.

Figure 1.52

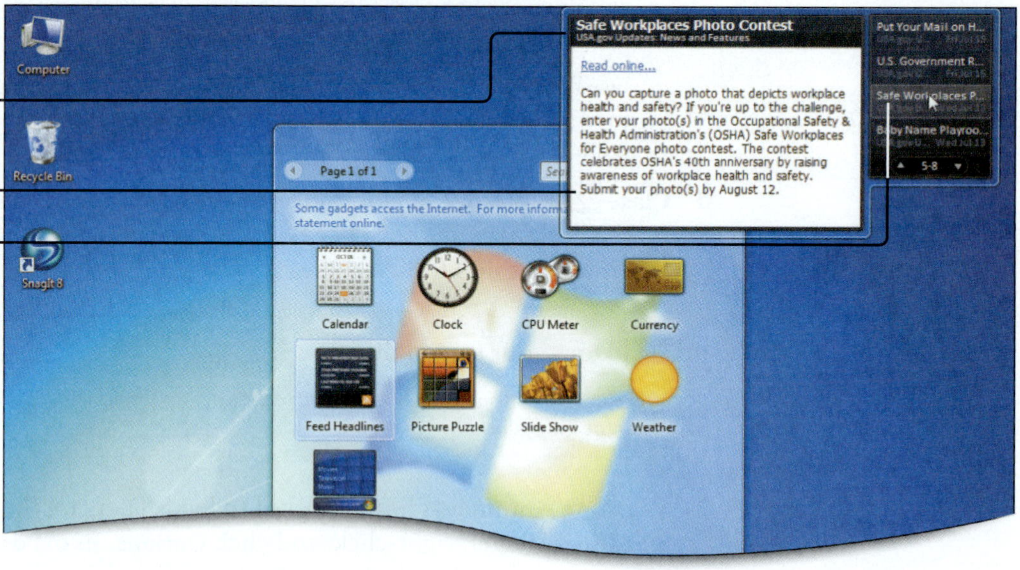

9 Click on the desktop to cancel the headline display.

10 **Start** the **Snipping Tool** program and create a **Full-screen Snip**. **Save** the snip in your **IE9 Chapter 1** folder as a **JPEG file** with the name **Lastname_Firstname_1B_RSS_Snip** **Close** the **Snipping Tool** window. Hold this file until you complete Project 1B, and then submit it as directed by your instructor.

11 Point to the gadget on your desktop and right-click. Click **Close gadget** to remove it from your desktop. **Close** the Gadgets window.

12 On the taskbar, click the **Internet Explorer** button. In the upper right corner, click the **View favorites, feeds, and history** button, and then if necessary, click the **Feeds tab**.

13 Point to the **USA.gov Updates** feed and right-click. Click **Delete**, and then click **Yes**.

14 **Close** Internet Explorer.

More Knowledge | What else should I know about RSS Feeds?

Feeds are different than a Web site: A feed can have the same content as a Web page, but the feed is usually formatted differently—in the form of headline topics. Additionally, when you subscribe to a feed, Internet Explorer automatically checks the Web site and downloads new content so you can see what is new since you last visited the feed.

The downside of seeing a feed instead of the actual Web site is that you do not get to benefit from the design of the Web page itself, where the format of the information or the photos and graphics could add to or possibly change your interpretation of the information.

Feeds are usually free: It is usually free to subscribe to a feed.

Other programs can display your feeds: Internet Explorer provides the Common Feed List to other programs, so you can subscribe to feeds with Internet Explorer and then read them in other programs such as your e-mail client or in one of the feed readers available as a gadget.

Feeds come in two common formats: Two common formats for feeds are RSS and Atom. Feed formats are constantly being updated with new versions, and Internet Explorer supports most RSS and Atom versions. All feed formats are based on XML (Extensible Markup Language), which is a text-based computer language used to describe and distribute structured data and documents.

Objective 9 | Use Web Slices, Accelerators, and Suggested Sites

An RSS feed enables you to get frequently changing content automatically by subscribing to the feed. A technology that is similar to, and based on, RSS technology, is a Web Slice. Recall that a Web Slice is a specific *portion*—a slice—of a Web page to which you can subscribe, and which enables you to see when updated content, such as the current temperature or the score of a particular sports team, is available from a site.

The ***Accelerators*** feature displays a blue Accelerator icon when you select text from any Web page, which when clicked enables you to accomplish tasks such as finding a map, defining a word, or e-mailing content to others.

Activity 1.14 | Using Web Slices

After you subscribe to a Web Slice, it displays as a link on the Favorites bar. When the Web Slice is updated, the link displays in bold, at which time you can click the link to see the updated content.

A Web Slice is useful for gathering up-to-date information that's important to you, such as weather, traffic, finance, and sports scores.

Another Way

If displayed on your Favorites bar, click Web Slices or Get More Add-ons; or, display the Manage Add-ons dialog box, and click *Find more toolbars and extensions.*

1 **Close** any open windows. On the taskbar, click the **Internet Explorer** button, click in the **address bar**, type **ieaddons.com** and then press Enter. In the toolbar near the top of the screen, click **add-ons**. Scroll to the bottom of the page, click the **Get Add-ons arrow**, and then click **Web Slices**. Compare your screen with Figure 1.53.

Figure 1.53

Web Slice thumbnails (yours may vary)

Web Slices selected

2 Near the upper right of the window, click **Search**, and then type **espn** and press Enter. Click the **ESPN: MLB Teams** thumbnail, and then click the **Add to Internet Explorer** button. When the **ESPN** site opens, on the **Command bar**, click the **Add Web Slices arrow**, and then click **ESPN: Tigers**.

3 In the **Internet Explorer** dialog box, click the **Add to Favorites bar** button. If necessary, Close the ESPN tab to leave only one tab open. Click in the **address bar**, type **weatherbug.com** press Enter, and then in the **Enter City or U.S. ZIP** search box, type **48103** Press Enter. In the **address bar**, type **usa.gov** to move to the U.S. Government page.

The weather for Ann Arbor, Michigan displays, and in the Command bar, the Add Web Slices button displays in green, indicating that a Web Slice is available for that page.

4 Click the **Add Web Slices arrow**, and then, at the top of the list, click the displayed temperature. In the **Internet Explorer** dialog box, click the **Add to Favorites bar** button. In the upper portion of your screen, notice that two Web Slices display in the Favorites bar.

5 In the **Favorites bar**, click the **ESPN: Tigers** button. Notice that the most recent information about the Tigers baseball team displays. Compare your screen with Figure 1.54.

When you click on a Web Slice, you do not navigate to a new page; rather a small *slice* of another Web page displays in a small window that you can quickly close. Or, you can click any link in the small window to navigate to the actual site.

Figure 1.54

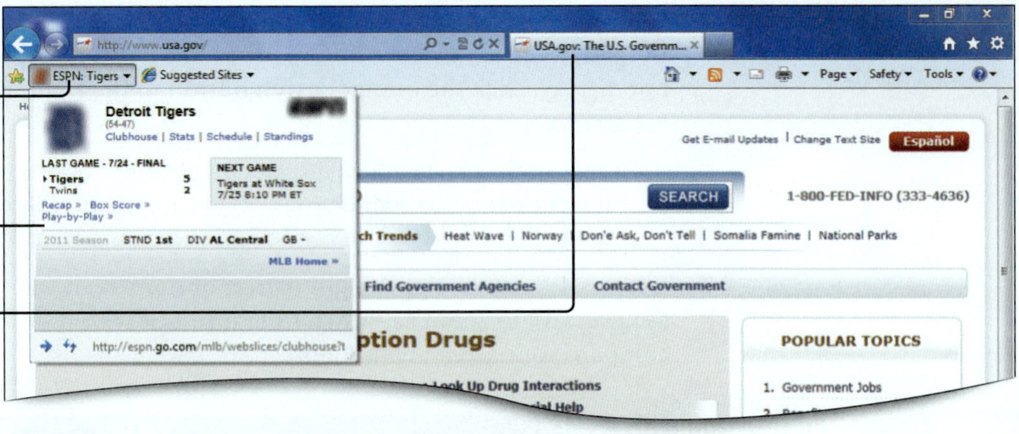

6 Click in a blank area of the screen to close the small window.

The next time the weather conditions change, or there is news about the Tigers, the appropriate link will display in bold, and you can view the updated information.

7 **Start** the **Snipping Tool** program and create a **Full-screen Snip**. **Save** the snip in your **IE9 Chapter 1** folder as a **JPEG file** with the name **Lastname_Firstname_1B_Slices_Snip Close** the **Snipping Tool** window. Hold this file until you complete Project 1B, and then submit it as directed by your instructor.

8 On the **Favorites bar**, point to the **WeatherBug** link, right-click, click **Delete**, and then click **Yes**. Repeat this procedure to delete the **ESPN** link.

You can add and delete Web Slices as you need them.

9 **Close** all Internet Explorer windows.

Activity 1.15 | Using Accelerators

To use an Accelerator, select some appropriate text on a Web page, click the blue Accelerator button, and then select the appropriate service, such as searching, mapping, shopping, or language translation.

1 On the taskbar, click the **Internet Explorer** button, click in the **address bar**, type **www.pasadena.edu** and then press Enter.

2 In the site's navigation bar, click **Apply & Register**, and then scroll to the bottom of the page.

3 Select the **address** of **Pasadena City College**, and then compare your screen with Figure 1.55. Notice that a **blue Accelerator** button displays.

Figure 1.55

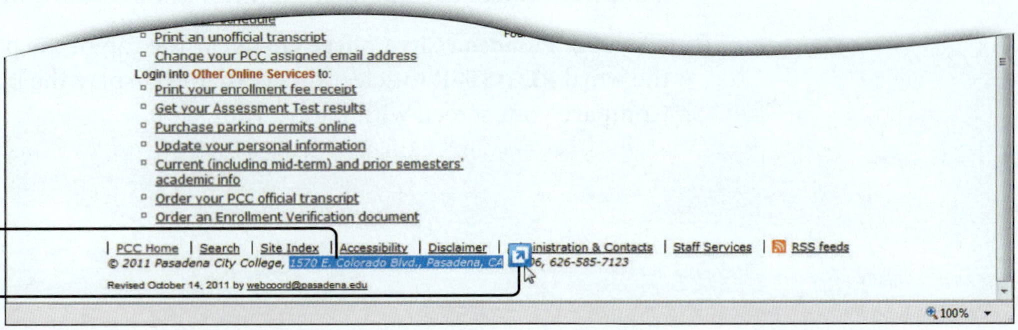

4 Click the **blue Accelerator** button to display a shortcut menu, and then click **Map with Bing**. If necessary, Maximize the window. If a map with the street address does not display, click the orange search button to the right of the address near the top of the screen.

A map of the street address displays. In the Bing mapping application, you can click various views of the address you selected, for example Bird's eye displays an overhead picture of the address.

5 If necessary, in the upper right corner of the screen, click the + button as many times as necessary to zoom as shown in Figure 1.56. *Point* to the **Bird's eye arrow**, and then compare your screen with Figure 1.56.

Figure 1.56

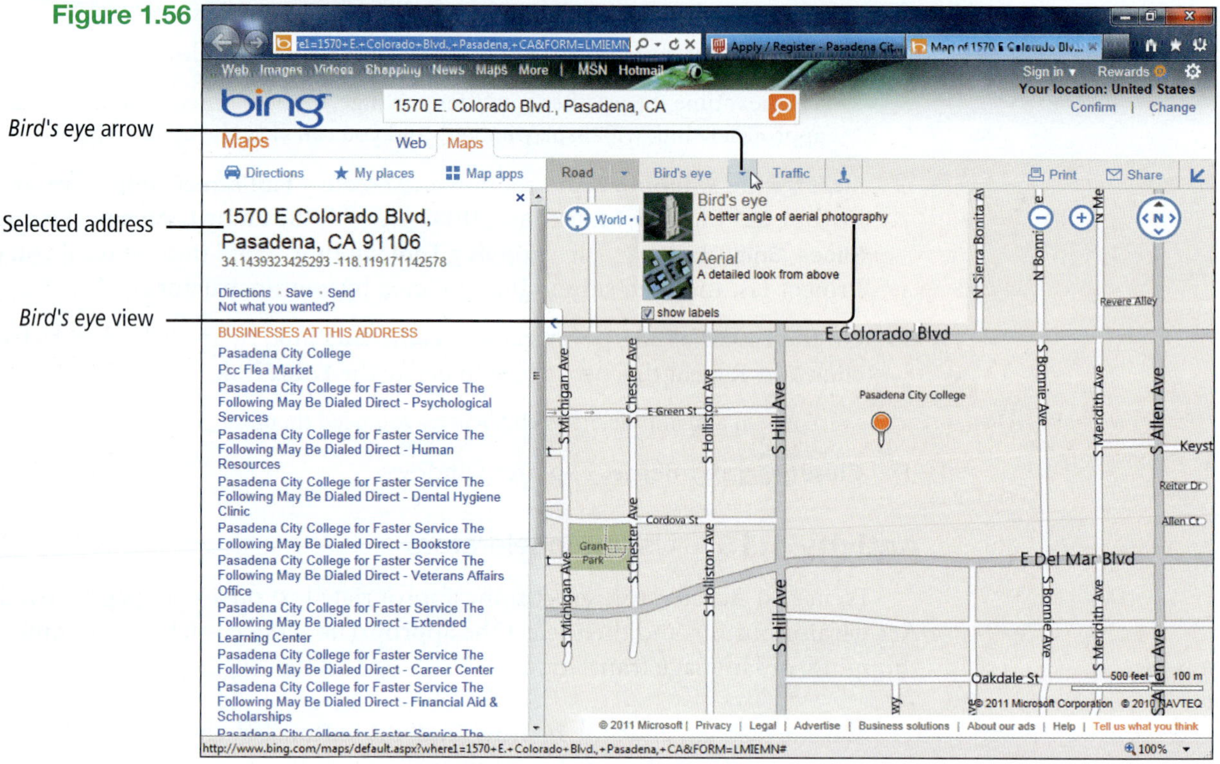

6 On the displayed list, click **Bird's eye**.

7 **Start** the **Snipping Tool** program and create a **Full-screen Snip**. **Save** the snip in your **IE9 Chapter 1** folder as a **JPEG file** with the name **Lastname_Firstname_1B_Accelerator_Snip Close** the **Snipping Tool** window. Hold this file until you complete Project 1B, and then submit it as directed by your instructor.

8 Click the **Pasadena City College tab**. Near the top of the page, locate and double-click the word **REGISTER** to select the word and display the blue Accelerator button. Compare your screen with Figure 1.57.

Figure 1.57

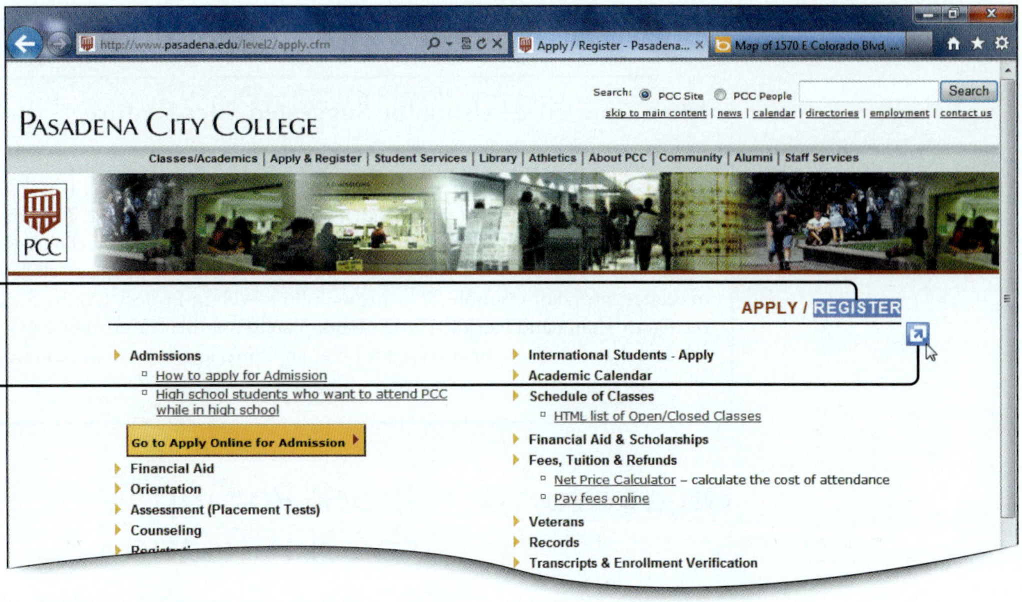

9 Click the **blue Accelerator** button, point to **All Accelerators**, and then click **Translate with Bing**. In the **Translate from** box, be sure *English* is selected. In the **Translate to** box, click the **arrow**, and then click **Spanish**. Click the orange **Translate** button, and then compare your screen with Figure 1.58.

Bing displays the translated word in the box on the left, and then displays the translation and definitions in the box on the right.

Figure 1.58

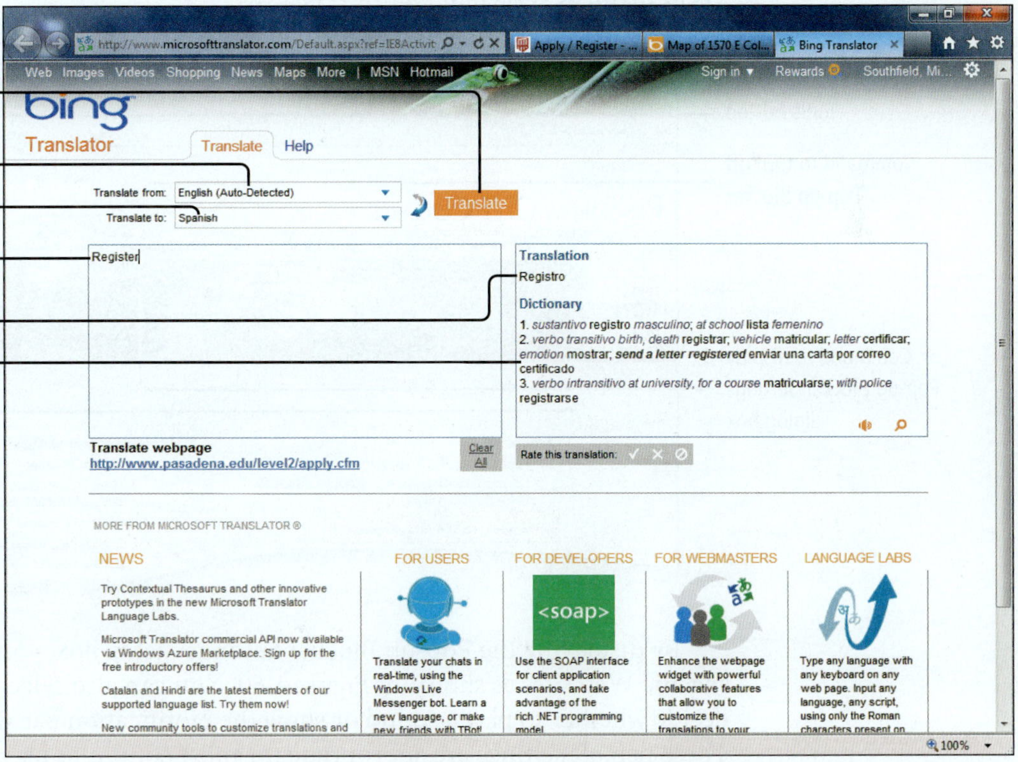

10 **Close** [Close button] all Internet Explorer windows.

> **More Knowledge | Using the Suggested Sites Feature**
>
> ***Suggested Sites*** is an optional online service that suggests other Web sites in which you might be interested based on the Web sites you visit most. First, you must activate the feature by clicking *Suggested Sites* on the Favorites bar. Then, click *Get your own suggestions*, and then click *Turn on Suggested Sites*—your procedure may differ. Or, from the Tools menu, click Suggested Sites, and then click Yes. Once activated, your Web browsing history is sent to Microsoft. Then, as you browse the Web, you can click the Suggested Sites link to see a list of related sites. For example, after browsing the Web in Project 1A, the feature might suggest additional sites related to Miami and Florida. If you do not plan to use this feature, you can right-click the link on the Favorites bar and delete it. You can also turn it off at any time, and even if activated, it does not record any information when InPrivate Browsing is turned on.

Objective 10 | Block Pop-up Windows and Use the Notification Bar

A ***pop-up*** is a small Web browser window that displays on top of the Web site you are viewing; pop-ups are usually created by advertisers. ***Pop-up Blocker*** is a feature in Internet Explorer that enables you to limit or block most pop-ups. The Notification bar displays information about downloads, blocked pop-up windows, add-ons, and other activities.

Activity 1.16 | Using the Internet Explorer 9 Pop-up Blocker and Notification Bar

Pop-up Blocker is enabled by default. To turn it off or change the settings, display the Tools menu as shown in Figure 1.59.

Figure 1.59

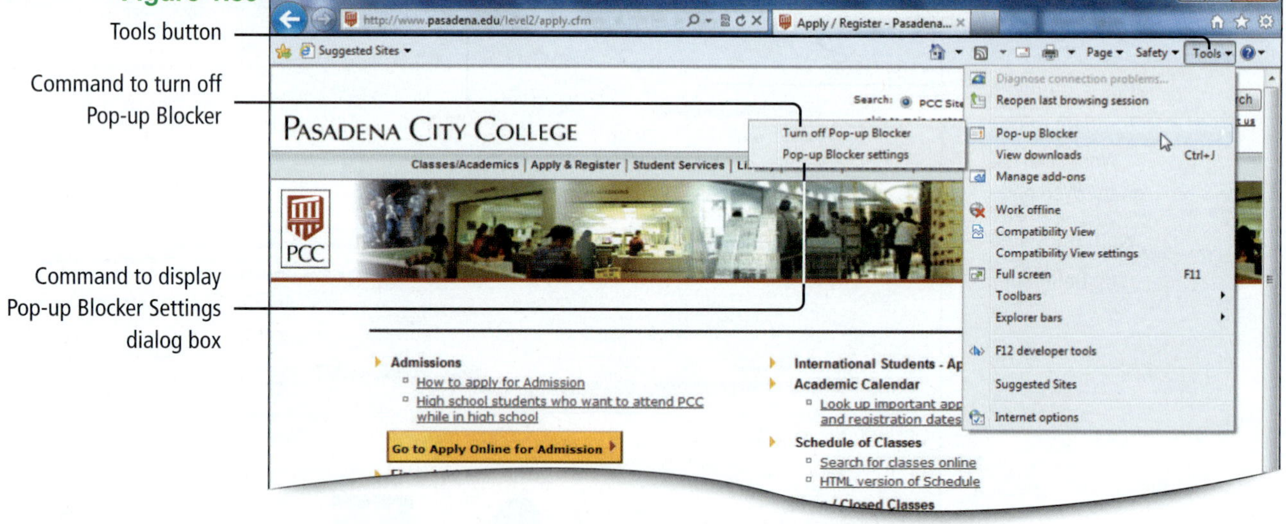

By displaying the Pop-up Blocker Settings dialog box, you can *allow* pop-ups from specific Web sites as shown in Figure 1.60. You can also select the Blocking level and decide whether to play a sound or show the Notification bar when a pop-up is blocked. These default settings are appropriate for most computer users. Some sites request that you allow pop-ups from their site, and if you trust the site, it is safe to do so. For example, the learning management system known as *Blackboard*, which is used by many colleges and universities, requests that you allow pop-ups from its site.

Figure 1.60

Pop-up Blocker Settings dialog box

Add allowed sites here

Allowed sites listed here

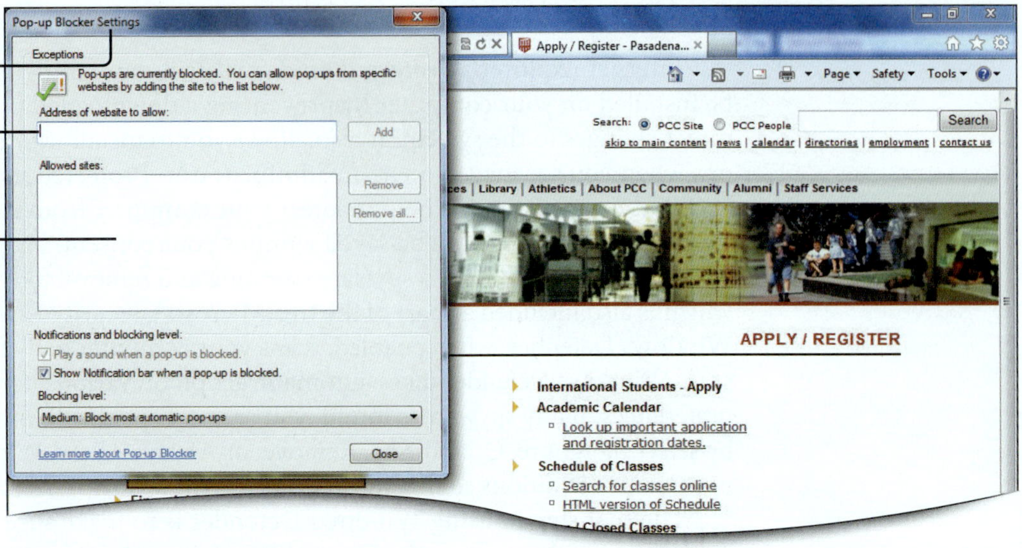

Because the Notification bar displays on a site when a pop-up is blocked, you always have the choice of viewing the pop-up message if you want to do so. Click the Notification bar and then click Show Blocked Pop-up. From the Notification bar, you can also click to temporarily accept pop-ups from a specific site.

The Notification bar will display at the bottom of the screen if:

- A site tries to install an ActiveX control, install an updated ActiveX control, install an add-on program, run an ActiveX control in an unsafe manner, or run active content.
- A site tries to download a file to your computer.
- Your security settings are below the recommended levels.
- You started Internet Explorer with add-ons disabled.

One advantage of the Notification bar is that you are not required to attend to it. For example, if you want to proceed without responding to the message, you can close the Notification bar. If you want to proceed with using a feature of the displayed site, click the message and then take appropriate action. For more information about the types of messages that you might see in the Notification bar, display the Windows Help and Support window, and search for *notification bar*.

To check how well you can identify pop-up blocking functions, take a moment to answer the following questions:

1 By default, Pop-up Blocker is __________.

2 You always have the choice of __________ a pop-up message if you want to do so.

3 One common reason that the Notification bar will display is if a Web site tries to install, update, or run in an unsafe manner any type of __________ control.

4 The Notification bar commonly displays if a site tries to __________ a file to your computer.

5 One advantage of the Notification bar is that you can __________ it if the message does not apply to what you want to do.

Objective 11 | Protect Against Malware

Internet Explorer will warn you when Web pages try to install software by displaying the Notification bar. There are additional ways in which Internet Explorer provides safety features to protect your computer against malware.

Activity 1.17 | Protecting Against Malware

Internet Explorer's ***protected mode*** makes it more difficult for malicious software to be installed on your computer by preventing a downloaded program from making any direct changes to the system. It also allows you to install *wanted* ActiveX controls or add-ons when you are logged on as an administrator. Protected mode is on by default. One way that protected mode helps protect your computer from malicious downloads is by restricting where files can be saved without your consent.

Windows Defender is a spyware scanning and removal tool included with Windows 7, which is also included as part of the free Microsoft Security Essentials package. By default, Windows Defender, when enabled, scans your computer daily for spyware. During the scan, Windows Defender takes automatic action on various items, depending on your preferences. If any spyware is found, you are prompted with options to deal with each threat by selecting Ignore, Quarantine, Remove, or Always Allow. Windows Defender constantly updates its definitions so that it can find new spyware threats that emerge on the Internet.

The first step in using Windows Defender is to make sure it is enabled on your computer. To do so, open the Control Panel, type *defender* in the Search box, and then click Windows Defender. To enable Windows Defender, click the *click here to turn it on* link, as shown in Figure 1.61, and then follow directions. If you are using another spyware scanning software program, or if you are using Microsoft Security Essentials—which includes both a spyware protection program and a built-in version of Windows Defender—you do not need to turn on a separate version of Windows Defender.

Figure 1.61

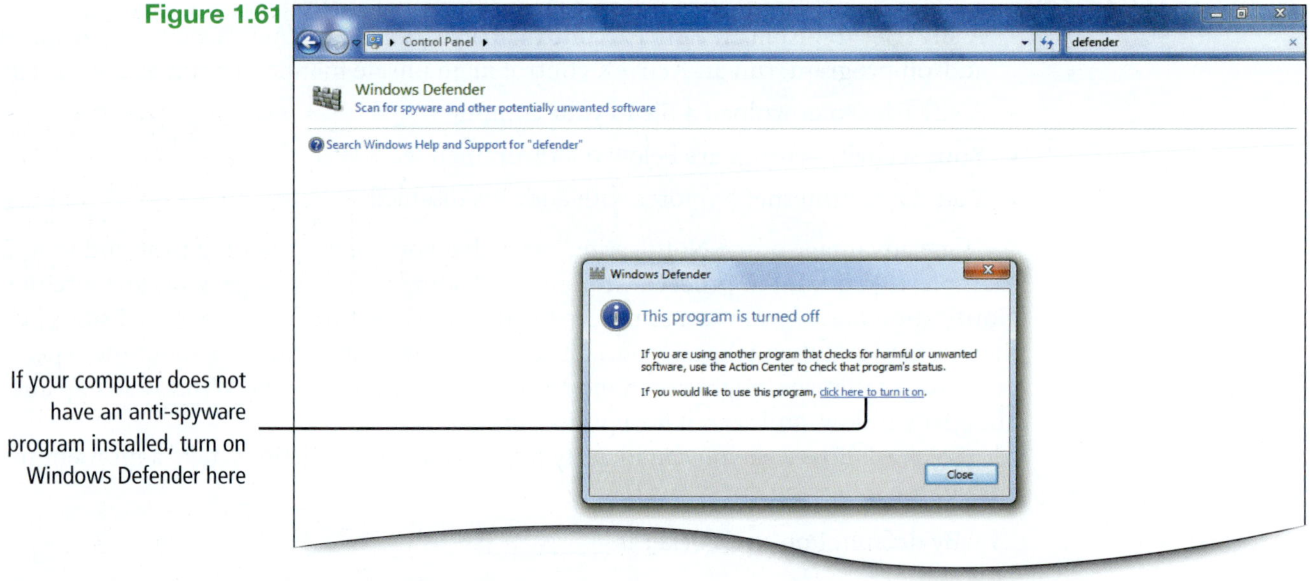

To check how well you understand protecting against malware, take a moment to answer the following questions:

1. Protected mode makes it difficult for malicious software to be installed on your computer by preventing a downloaded program from making direct _________ to the system.
2. Protected mode is on by _________.
3. Protected mode restricts where a downloaded file can be stored without your _________.
4. When enabled, Windows Defender scans your computer for _________ daily.
5. Windows Defender constantly updates its _________ so that it can find new spyware threats that emerge on the Internet.

Objective 12 | Protect Your Data

Windows 7 provides a variety of ways to protect your personal data and your electronic transactions.

Activity 1.18 | Protecting Your Data

A ***certificate*** is a digital document that verifies the identity of a person or indicates the security of a Web site. Certificates are issued by trusted companies known as ***Certification Authorities***. Certificates make secure transactions on the Internet possible. When you visit a secure Web site in Internet Explorer, a padlock icon will display in the address bar indicating that a digital certificate identifies the site, and the address bar will typically display in green. As shown in Figure 1.62, you can click the padlock icon to display information about the certificate.

Figure 1.62

Secure site address bar displays in green

Padlock icon in address bar

Information about the certificate

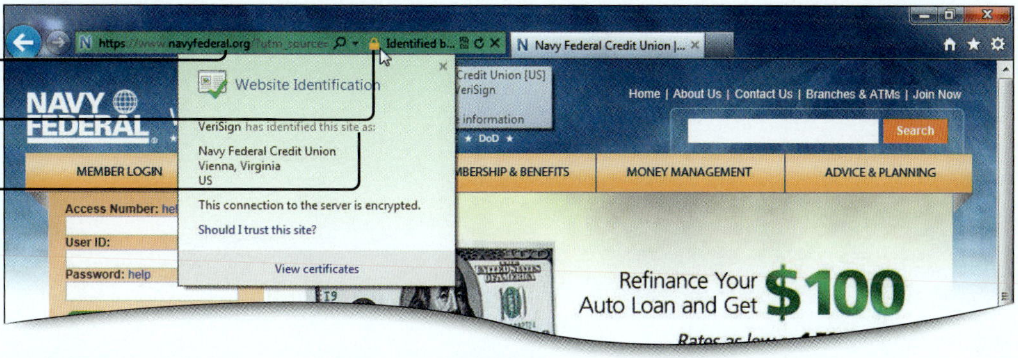

You can see specific information about the issuer of the certificate by clicking *View certificates*. You will commonly see such certificate information on any site where financial transactions are involved.

Phishing is a technique used to trick computer users into revealing personal or financial information through an e-mail message or a Web site. The message or site appears to come from a trusted source but actually directs recipients to provide information to a fraudulent Web site.

SmartScreen Filter is a feature in Internet Explorer that helps detect phishing Web sites and Web sites that distribute malware. SmartScreen Filter runs in the background and protects you by comparing the addresses of Web sites you visit against a list of sites reported to Microsoft as legitimate. This list is stored on your computer. It also analyzes the sites you visit to see if they have characteristics common to a phishing site.

To manually check a Web site that you find suspicious, navigate to the site you want to check. On the Command bar, click Safety, point to SmartScreen Filter, click *Check this website*, and then click OK. If a Web site is flagged as suspicious, you should not submit any personal or financial information to it unless you are certain that the site is trustworthy. Suspicious sites are flagged by Internet Explorer by displaying the address bar in yellow along with a message. For more information about how Internet Explorer handles phishing, in the Windows Help and Support window, search for *phishing* and click SmartScreen Filter: frequently asked questions.

To check how well you understand data protection, take a moment to answer the following questions:

1 A certificate can verify the _________ of a Web site.

2 Certificates make _________ transactions on the Web possible.

3 When you visit a secure Web site, the address bar displays a _________ icon.

4 A technique to trick computer users into revealing personal information is _________.

5 If the SmartScreen Filter in Internet Explorer suspects a Web site of having phishing characteristics, it will display a message and display the address bar in _________.

End **You have completed Project 1B**

Content-Based Assessments

Summary

In this chapter, you used tabbed browsing to open multiple Web sites in a single browser window. You created and organized Favorites. When you use public computers, it is a good idea to delete your browsing history, which you practiced in this chapter. You also practiced printing and saving information on a Web page.

In this chapter, you practiced locating, subscribing to, and viewing RSS feeds. You also practiced how to use Web Slices and Accelerators. There are many excellent search providers that you can use to search the Web, and in this chapter, you used several providers to search.

Key Terms

Accelerators 41
ActiveX 32
ActiveX control 32
Add-on 31
Address bar 3
Blog 3
Bookmark managers 20
Browsing 3
Browsing history 20
Certificate 49
Certification Authorities 49
Command bar 22
Cookies 21
Country codes 5
Digital signature 32
Domain name 5
Favorites bar 19
Favorites Center 15
Feed reader 38
Home page 3
http 5
HyperText Transfer Protocol 5
InPrivate Browsing 23
Internet Explorer 9 3
Navigation bar 11
New Tab page 6
Notification bar 31
Phishing 49
Pop-up 46
Pop-up Blocker 46
Portal 24
Protected mode 48
Protocol prefix 5
RSS 37
RSS feed 37
RSS viewer 38
Search provider 35
Search term 35
Show Address bar Autocomplete 6
SmartScreen Filter 49
Sponsored links 35
Suggested Sites 46
Surfing 3
Syndicated content ... 37
Tab row 4
Tabbed browsing 3
Tear-off tab 13
Temporary Internet files 21
Top level domain 5
Uniform Resource Locator 3
URL 3
Web browser 3
Web feed 37
Web log 3
Web Slice 19
Windows Defender 48
XML feed 37

Matching

Match each term in the second column with its correct definition in the first column. Write the letter of the term on the blank line in front of the correct definition.

_____ 1. Any software program with which you display Web pages and navigate the Internet.

_____ 2. The Web browser software developed by Microsoft Corporation that is included with Windows 7.

_____ 3. The term used to describe the process of using your computer to view Web pages.

_____ 4. A feature in Internet Explorer that enables you to open multiple Web sites in a single browser window.

_____ 5. The area across the upper portion of the Internet Explorer window in which a tab for each open Web site displays.

_____ 6. A feature in Internet Explorer that makes it more difficult for malicious software to be installed on your computer by preventing a downloaded program from making any direct changes to the system.

A Accelerators
B Browsing
C Cookies
D Favorites bar
E Favorites Center
F InPrivate Browsing
G Internet Explorer 9
H Pop-up
I Protected mode
J RSS feed
K Search term

____ 7.	A list of links to Web sites that is saved in your Web browser.	**L** Tab row
____ 8.	A toolbar in Internet Explorer 9 that displays directly below the address bar and to which you can add or drag Web addresses you use frequently.	**M** Tabbed browsing
____ 9.	Small text files that Web sites put on your computer to store information about you and your preferences, for example logon information.	**N** Web browser
____ 10.	A feature in Internet Explorer 9 with which you can browse the Web without storing data about your browsing session.	**O** Web Slice
____ 11.	A word or phrase that describes the topic about which you want to find information.	
____ 12.	Frequently updated content published by a Web site and delivered to a feed reader.	
____ 13.	A specific *portion*—a slice—of a Web page to which you can subscribe, and which enables you to see when updated content, such as the current temperature, is available from a site.	
____ 14.	An Internet Explorer feature that displays a blue button when you select text from any Web page, from which you can accomplish tasks such as finding a map or defining a word.	
____ 15.	A small Web browser window that displays on top of the Web site you are viewing, and which is usually created by advertisers.	

Multiple Choice

Circle the correct answer.

1. An online journal or column used to publish personal or company information is a:
a. web feed **b.** blog **c.** search provider

2. The ending letters of a URL such as *.com*, *.org*, and so on is the:
a. locator **b.** country code **c.** top level domain

3. A Web site that displays news, content, and links that are of interest to a specific audience is a:
a. portal **b.** URL **c.** feed

4. Frequently updated content published by a Web site and delivered to a feed reader is:
a. an RSS feed **b.** a blog **c.** a cookie

5. Programs that add features to a Web browser such as Internet Explorer are:
a. bookmark managers **b.** temporary Internet files **c.** add-ons

6. A Web site that provides search capabilities on the Web is called a:
a. sponsored link **b.** search provider **c.** domain

7. An example of an Accelerator is a:
a. domain name **b.** digital signature **c.** mapping site

8. A feature in Internet Explorer that makes it difficult for malicious software to be installed on your computer is:
a. protected mode **b.** syndicated content **c.** ActiveX

9. A spyware scanning and removal tool included with Windows 7 is:
a. Windows Blocker **b.** Windows Defender **c.** Windows Security

10. A technique used to trick computer users into revealing personal information is:
a. hacking **b.** spying **c.** phishing

Apply **1A** skills from these Objectives:

1 Use Tabbed Browsing
2 Organize Favorites
3 Manage Browsing History and Browse with InPrivate
4 Print, Zoom, and Change the Text Size of Web Pages
5 Save Web Page Information
6 Manage Add-ons

Skills Review | Project 1C Browsing the Web with Internet Explorer 9

Project Files

For Project 1C, you will need the following files:

The student data files that accompany this textbook, which you can download from the Companion Web Site at www.pearsonhighered.com/go
IE901_1C_Answer_Sheet (Word document)

You will save your document as:

Lastname_Firstname_1C_Answer_Sheet

1 **Close** all open windows. On the taskbar, click the **Windows Explorer** button. In the **navigation pane**, click the drive that contains the student files that you downloaded for this textbook. Locate and double-click the Word file **IE901_1C_Answer_Sheet** to open Word and display the document, and then close the folder containing your student files. Press F12 to display the **Save As** dialog box in Word, navigate to your **IE9 Chapter1** folder, and then using your own name, save the document as **Lastname_Firstname_1C_Answer_Sheet** If necessary, click OK if a message regarding formats displays.

On the taskbar, click the **Word** button to minimize the window and leave your Word document accessible from the taskbar. As you complete each step in this project, click the Word button on the taskbar to open the document, type your one-letter answer in the appropriate cell of the Word table, and then on the taskbar, click the button again to minimize the window for the next step.

Open Internet Explorer. Click in the **address bar** and navigate to **doh.state.fl.us** Open a **New Tab**, and then go to the site **miamigov.com** On a **New Tab**, go to the site **hsmv.state.fl.us** On the **taskbar**, point to the **Internet Explorer** button. What is your result?

- **a.** Thumbnails for each open site display.
- **b.** A list of recently visited Web sites displays.
- **c.** The tabs in the tab row are rearranged in alphabetical order.

2 To the right of the **tab row**, click the **Home** button. What is your result?

- **a.** The default Home page opens in another tab.
- **b.** The default Home page opens, and all other tabs are closed.
- **c.** The default Home page opens in the active tab window.

3 On a **New Tab**, go to the site **florida.edu** and then click the **View favorites, feeds, and history** button. Click **Add to favorites**. What is your result?

- **a.** The Favorites Center pane displays on the right side of the screen.
- **b.** The Create Favorites Folder dialog box displays.
- **c.** The Add a Favorite dialog box displays.

4 Click **Cancel**. On the displayed home page for **Florida International University**, on the **navigation bar**, point to the link for **Athletics** and then right-click. From the displayed shortcut menu, which of the following actions are possible?

- **a.** You can open the Athletics link in a new tab.
- **b.** You can send the Athletics link to your Documents folder.
- **c.** You can create a tab group.

5 Click in a blank area of the screen to close the shortcut menu. Click the **View favorites, feeds, and history** button to open the **Favorites Center** pane. Across the top of this pane, which tabs display?

- **a.** Favorites, Tab Groups, Feeds
- **b.** Favorites, Feeds, History
- **c.** Favorites, History, Recent Pages

6 Click the **History tab**, and then click the **arrow**. Which of the following is *not* a viewing arrangement?

- **a.** By Date
- **b.** By Favorites
- **c.** By Most Visited

(Project 1C Browsing the Web with Internet Explorer 9 continues on the next page)

Skills Review | Project 1C Browsing the Web with Internet Explorer 9 (continued)

7 Click in a blank area of the screen to close the **Favorites Center** pane. On the **Command bar**, click the **Safety** button, and then click **Delete browsing history**. According to this information, cookies consist of:

a. Saved information that you have typed into forms.

b. Buttons added to the tab row.

c. Files stored on your computer by Web sites to save preferences.

8 **Close** the **Delete Browsing History** dialog box. Click the **Tools** button, and then click **Manage Add-ons**. At the bottom of the screen, click **Find more toolbars and extensions**. What is your result?

a. A list of add-ons stored on your computer displays.

b. A list of recently used add-ons displays.

c. The Microsoft site for finding and installing new add-ons displays.

9 **Close** the **Add-ons** site and the **Manage Add-ons** dialog box. Click the **New Tab** button. Click the **Safety** button, and then click **InPrivate Browsing**. What is your result?

a. The Delete Browsing History dialog box displays.

b. InPrivate displays in the address bar.

c. Both A and B.

10 **Close** the **InPrivate** window. Display the **FIU** site, click the **Print button arrow**, and then click **Print preview**. Click the **Page Setup** button to display the Page Setup dialog box. From this dialog box, which of the following can be changed?

a. Left and right margins

b. Headers and footers

c. Both A and B

Be sure you have typed all of your answers in your Word document. **Save** and **Close** your Word document, and submit as directed by your instructor. **Close** all open windows.

End **You have completed Project 1C**

Apply **1B** skills from these Objectives:

7 Search the Internet
8 Subscribe to and View an RSS Feed
9 Use Web Slices, Accelerators, and Suggested Sites
10 Block Pop-up Windows and Use the Notification Bar
11 Protect Against Malware
12 Protect Your Data

Skills Review | Project 1D Searching with Search Tools and Using the Web Safely

Project Files

For Project 1D, you will need the following files:

The student data files that accompany this textbook, which you can download from the Companion Web Site at www.pearsonhighered.com/go
IE901_1D_Answer_Sheet (Word document)

You will save your document as:

Lastname_Firstname_1D_Answer_Sheet

1 **Close** all open windows. On the taskbar, click the **Windows Explorer** button. In the **navigation pane**, click the drive that contains the student files that you downloaded for this textbook. Locate and double-click the Word file **IE901_1D_Answer_Sheet** to open Word and display the document, and then close the folder containing your student files. Press F12 to display the **Save As** dialog box in Word, navigate to your **IE9 Chapter 1** folder, and then using your own name, save the document as **Lastname_Firstname_1D_Answer_Sheet** If necessary, click OK if a message regarding formats displays.

On the taskbar, click the **Word** button to minimize the window and leave your Word document accessible from the taskbar. As you complete each step in this project, click the Word button on the taskbar to open the document, type your one-letter answer in the appropriate cell of the Word table, and then on the taskbar, click the button again to minimize the window for the next step.

Close Internet Explorer if it is open, and then **Start** Internet Explorer again. Click the **Tools** button, and then click **Manage add-ons**. Click **Search Providers**, select **Bing**, and if necessary, set **Bing** as the default. **Close** the Manage Add-ons dialog box. In the address bar, type **florida education** and press Enter. What is your result?

- **a.** A Bing search is conducted using *florida education* as a search term.
- **b.** The FloridaEducation.com Web site displays.
- **c.** A message box displays a *Web site not found* message.

2 Display the **Manage add-ons** dialog box again, display the list of search providers, and then at the bottom, click **Find more search providers**. What is your result?

- **a.** A list of recently used search providers displays.
- **b.** The Microsoft site for adding search providers to Internet Explorer 9 displays.
- **c.** Bing conducts an Internet search for search providers.

3 Locate the **New York Times Instant Search**, point to the logo that indicates *The New York Times*, right-click, and then click **Save picture as**. What is your result?

- **a.** An error message indicates that you cannot save this as a picture.
- **b.** The logo displays in Windows Photo Viewer.
- **c.** The Save Picture dialog box displays.

4 Click **Cancel** to close the dialog box. In the categories of possible add-ons, click **Travel**. In the list at the bottom of the page, select **Search Providers**. Which of the following is true?

- **a.** The first Travel search provider in the list is opened.
- **b.** A short group of Travel search provider thumbnails displays.
- **c.** A search box displays, which enables you to further refine your search.

5 Click in the **address bar**, type **noaa.gov** and then press Enter. On this page, what signifies that an RSS Feed is available from this site?

- **a.** The Feeds button lights up in green.
- **b.** The Feeds button lights up in orange.
- **c.** The Feeds button blinks on and off.

6 On the **Command bar**, click the **Feeds** button. What is your result?

- **a.** The Feed Headlines gadget displays.
- **b.** The NOAA News Releases displays as a feed to which you can subscribe.
- **c.** The Feeds tab of the Favorites Center displays.

(Project 1D Searching with Search Tools and Using the Web Safely continues on the next page)

Skills Review | Project 1D Searching with Search Tools and Using the Web Safely (continued)

7 On the **Command bar**, click the **Tools** button, point to **Pop-up Blocker**, and then click **Pop-up Blocker settings**. What does the **Medium blocking level** do with pop-ups?

a. Allows pop-ups from secure sites

b. Blocks most automatic pop-ups

c. Blocks all pop-ups

8 What notifications are available to notify you when a pop-up has been blocked?

a. Play a sound

b. Display the Notification bar

c. Both A and B

9 **Close** the **Pop-up Blocker Settings** dialog box. From the **Start menu**, click **Help and Support**, and then in the **Search Help** box type **notification bar** and press Enter. In the displayed list, click **Internet Explorer 9 Notification bar: frequently asked questions**. Can you turn off the Notification bar?

a. Yes

b. No

c. Yes, but only for the current browser session

10 At the top of the **Windows Help and Support** window, delete the text *notification bar*, type **protected mode** and press Enter. Which of the following is *not* true about protected mode?

a. Protected mode is turned on by default.

b. Protected mode allows you to install wanted ActiveX controls or add-ons when you are logged on as an administrator.

c. Protected mode prevents you from entering credit card information into a Web site.

Be sure you have typed all of your answers in your Word document. **Save** and **Close** your Word document, and submit as directed by your instructor. **Close** all open windows.

End **You have completed Project 1D**

Content-Based Assessments

Apply 1A skills from these Objectives:

1. Use Tabbed Browsing
2. Organize Favorites
3. Manage Browsing History and Browse with InPrivate
4. Print, Zoom, and Change the Text Size of Web Pages
5. Save Web Page Information
6. Manage Add-ons

Mastering Internet Explorer 9 | Project 1E Browsing the Web with Internet Explorer 9

In the following Internet Explorer 9 project, you will open related sites on separate tabs. You will capture and save a screen that will look similar to Figure 1.63.

Project Files

For Project 1E, you will need the following file:

New Snip file

You will save your document as:

Lastname_Firstname_1E_Sites_Snip

Project Results

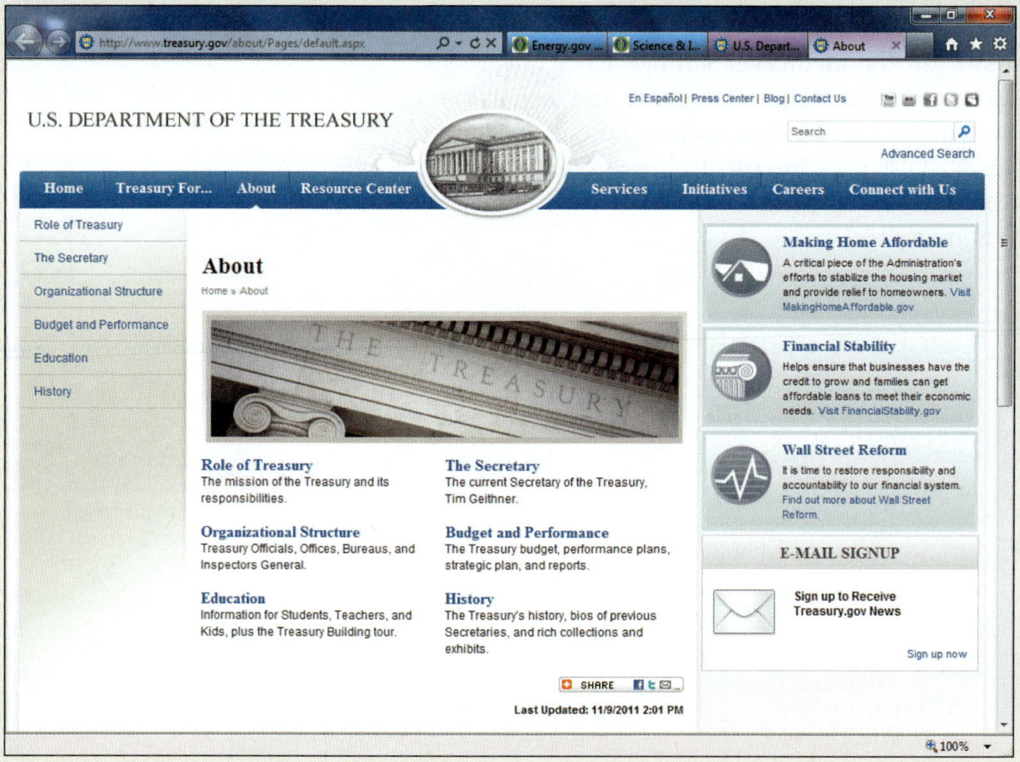

Figure 1.63

(Project 1E Browsing the Web with Internet Explorer 9 continues on the next page)

Mastering Internet Explorer 9 | Project 1E Browsing the Web with Internet Explorer 9 (continued)

1 Open Internet Explorer and be sure only the tab for your home page displays. Click in the **address bar**, type **www.doe.gov** and press Enter. Hold down Ctrl, and then in the navigation bar in this site, click **Science & Innovation** so that a new tab is created for the link and the two tabs are color coded.

2 On a **New Tab**, go to the site **www.treasury.gov** Hold down Ctrl, and then in the navigation bar of this site, click **About** so that a new tab is created for the link and the two tabs are color coded. Click the **About tab**.

3 Create a **Full-screen Snip**, and then **Save** the snip in your **IE9 Chapter 1** folder as a **JPEG file** with the name **Lastname_Firstname_1E_Sites_Snip** Submit this file as directed by your instructor.

4 **Close** all open windows and **Close** Internet Explorer.

End **You have completed Project 1E**

Apply 1B skills from these Objectives:

7 Search the Internet
8 Subscribe to and View an RSS Feed
9 Use Web Slices, Accelerators, and Suggested Sites
10 Block Pop-up Windows and Use the Notification Bar
11 Protect Against Malware
12 Protect Your Data

Mastering Internet Explorer 9 | Project 1F Searching with Search Tools and Using the Web Safely

In the following Internet Explorer 9 project, you will use an Accelerator. You will capture and save a screen that will look similar to Figure 1.64.

Project Files

For Project 1F, you will need the following file:

New Snip file

You will save your document as:

Lastname_Firstname_1F_Aerial_Snip

Project Results

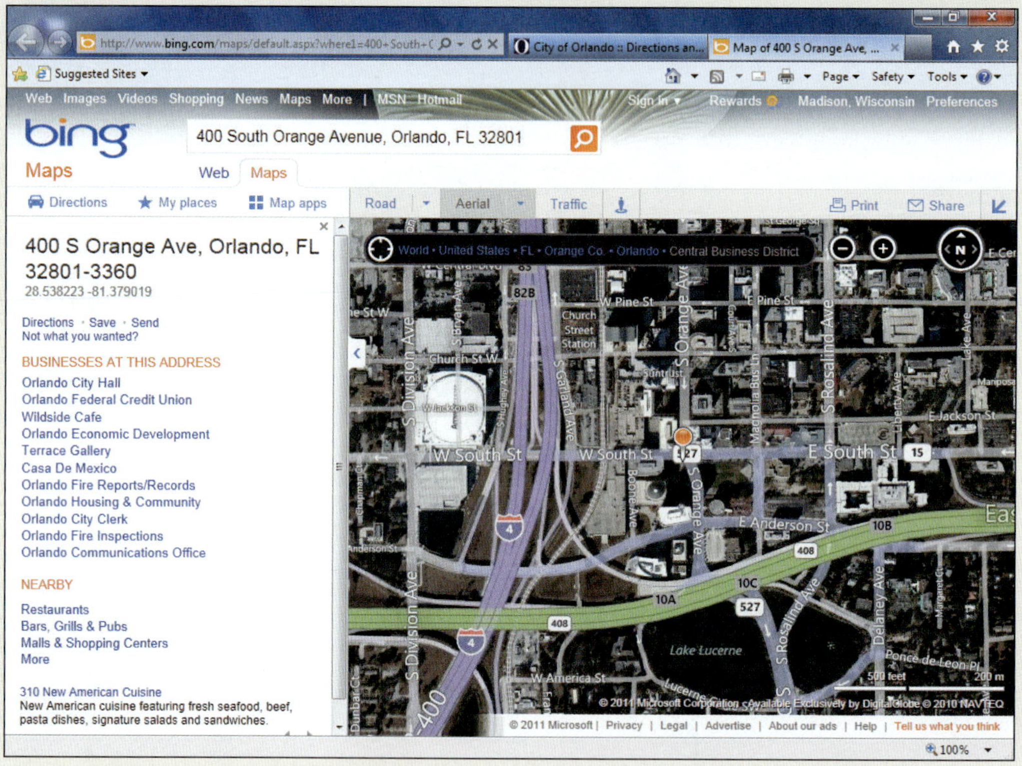

Figure 1.64

(Project 1F Searching with Search Tools and Using the Web Safely continues on the next page)

Mastering Internet Explorer 9 | Project 1F Searching with Search Tools and Using the Web Safely (continued)

1 Open Internet Explorer. In the **address bar**, type **www.cityoforlando.net** and press Enter. On the site's **Information Center** navigation bar, click **City Hall Hours & Directions**.

2 Select the City Hall address (include the city, state, and ZIP code), click the **Accelerator** button, and then click **Map with Bing**.

3 Set the view to **Aerial**. Create a **Full-screen Snip** and **Save** it as **Lastname_Firstname_1F_Aerial_Snip** Submit this file as directed by your instructor.

4 **Close** all open windows and **Close** Internet Explorer.

End **You have completed Project 1F**

Outcomes-Based Assessments

Rubric

The following outcomes-based assessments are open-ended assessments. That is, there is no specific correct result; your result will depend on your approach to the information provided. Make Professional Quality your goal. Use the following scoring rubric to guide you in how to approach the problem and then to evaluate how well your approach solves the problem.

The *criteria*—Software Mastery, Content, Format and Layout, and Process—represent the knowledge and skills you have gained that you can apply to solving the problem. The *levels of performance*—Professional Quality, Approaching Professional Quality, or Needs Quality Improvements—help you and your instructor evaluate your result.

	Your completed project is of Professional Quality if you:	**Your completed project is Approaching Professional Quality if you:**	**Your completed project Needs Quality Improvements if you:**
1-Software Mastery	Choose and apply the most appropriate skills, tools, and features and identify efficient methods to solve the problem.	Choose and apply some appropriate skills, tools, and features, but not in the most efficient manner.	Choose inappropriate skills, tools, or features, or are inefficient in solving the problem.
2-Content	Construct a solution that is clear and well organized, contains content that is accurate, appropriate to the audience and purpose, and is complete. Provide a solution that contains no errors in spelling, grammar, or style.	Construct a solution in which some components are unclear, poorly organized, inconsistent, or incomplete. Misjudge the needs of the audience. Have some errors in spelling, grammar, or style, but the errors do not detract from comprehension.	Construct a solution that is unclear, incomplete, or poorly organized; contains some inaccurate or inappropriate content; and contains many errors in spelling, grammar, or style. Do not solve the problem.
3-Format and Layout	Format and arrange all elements to communicate information and ideas, clarify function, illustrate relationships, and indicate relative importance.	Apply appropriate format and layout features to some elements, but not others. Overuse features, causing minor distraction.	Apply format and layout that does not communicate information or ideas clearly. Do not use format and layout features to clarify function, illustrate relationships, or indicate relative importance. Use available features excessively, causing distraction.
4-Process	Use an organized approach that integrates planning, development, self-assessment, revision, and reflection.	Demonstrate an organized approach in some areas, but not others; or, use an insufficient process of organization throughout.	Do not use an organized approach to solve the problem.

Apply a combination of the 1A and 1B skills.

Problem Solving | Project 1G Help Desk

Project Files

For Project 1G, you will need the following file:

IE901_1G_Help_Desk

You will save your document as:

Lastname_Firstname_1G_Help_Desk

From the student files that accompany this textbook, open the **Chapter_Files** folder, and then in the **Chapter_01** folder, locate and open the Word document **IE901_1G_Help_Desk**. Save the document in your chapter folder as **Lastname_Firstname_1G_Help_Desk**

The following e-mail question has arrived at the Help Desk from an employee at the Bell Orchid Hotel's corporate office. In the Word document, construct a response based on your knowledge of Internet Explorer 9. Although an e-mail response is not as formal as a letter, you should still use good grammar, good sentence structure, professional language, and a polite tone. Save your document and submit the response as directed by your instructor.

To: Help Desk

I have asked my research assistant to conduct some Internet research about what hotels around the country are doing in regard to designing innovative restaurants. Is there a way he could organize the sites he wants me to review by geographic location and by type of restaurant?

End **You have completed Project 1G**

Apply a combination of the 1A and 1B skills.

Problem Solving | Project 1H Help Desk

Project Files

For Project 1H, you will need the following file:

IE901_1H_Help_Desk

You will save your document as:

Lastname_Firstname_1H_Help_Desk

From the student files that accompany this textbook, open the **Chapter_Files** folder, and then in the **Chapter_01** folder, locate and open the Word document **IE901_1H_Help_Desk**. Save the document in your chapter folder as **Lastname_Firstname_1H_Help_Desk**

The following e-mail question has arrived at the Help Desk from an employee at the Bell Orchid Hotel's corporate office. In the Word document, construct a response based on your knowledge of Internet Explorer 9. Although an e-mail response is not as formal as a letter, you should still use good grammar, good sentence structure, professional language, and a polite tone. Save your document and submit the response as directed by your instructor.

To: Help Desk

Guests who use the computers in our hotel Business Centers have inquired about how they can prevent others from seeing the sites they visited and potentially seeing personal information. What instructions could we post at each of these computers to advise guests how to remove any such information from these public computers?

End **You have completed Project 1H**

Outcomes-Based Assessments

Apply a combination of the **1A** and **1B** skills.

Problem Solving | Project 1I Help Desk

Project Files

For Project 1I, you will need the following file:

IE901_1I_Help_Desk

You will save your document as:

Lastname_Firstname_1I_Help_Desk

From the student files that accompany this textbook, open the **Chapter_Files** folder, and then in the **Chapter_01** folder, locate and open the Word document **IE901_1I_Help_Desk**. Save the document in your chapter folder as **Lastname_Firstname_1I_Help_Desk**

The following e-mail question has arrived at the Help Desk from an employee at the Bell Orchid Hotel's corporate office. In the Word document, construct a response based on your knowledge of Internet Explorer 9. Although an e-mail response is not as formal as a letter, you should still use good grammar, good sentence structure, professional language, and a polite tone. Save your document and submit the response as directed by your instructor.

To: Help Desk

Guests commonly stop by the Front Desk at our hotels and inquire about what the weather will be like in the next few days. Is there a way we could have something on all of the Front Desk computers that would provide the Desk Clerks with constantly updated weather information?

End **You have completed Project 1I**

Glossary

Accelerators An Internet Explorer feature that displays a blue Accelerator icon when you select text from any Web page, and which when clicked enables you to accomplish tasks such as finding a map, defining a word, or e-mailing content to others.

ActiveX A technology for creating interactive Web content such as animation sequences, credit card transactions, or spreadsheet calculations.

ActiveX control A type of add-on that uses ActiveX technology.

Add-on A program that adds features to a Web browser such as Internet Explorer.

Address bar The area at the top of the Internet Explorer window that displays, and where you can type, a URL or a search term.

Blog An online journal or column used to publish personal or company information in an informal manner.

Bookmark managers Free Web tools available to manage your favorites.

Browsing The term used to describe the process of using your computer to view Web pages.

Browsing history The information stored by Internet Explorer about the sites you have visited and the information you have typed into a site.

Certificate A digital document that verifies the identity of a person or indicates the security of a Web site.

Certification Authorities Companies, for example Verisign, that issue digital certificates.

Command bar Contains the buttons to view your Home page, settings, and tools; view your feeds and mail; print Web pages; and get Help.

Cookies Small text files that Web sites put on your computer to store information about you and your preferences, for example logon information.

Country codes Top level domains for countries, for example *.ca* for Canada.

Digital signature An electronic security mark that can be added to files.

Domain name An organization's unique name on the Internet, which consists of a chosen name combined with a top level domain such as *.com* or *.org* or *.gov*.

Favorites bar A toolbar in Internet Explorer 9 that displays directly below the address bar and to which you can add or drag Web addresses you use frequently.

Favorites Center A list of links to Web sites that is saved in your Web browser.

Feed reader Another name for an RSS viewer.

Home page On your own computer, the Web page you have selected—or that is set by default—to display on your computer when you start Internet Explorer; when visiting a Web site, the starting point for the remainder of the pages on that site.

http The protocol prefix for HyperText Transfer Protocol.

HyperText Transfer Protocol The set of communication rules used by your computer to connect to servers on the Web.

InPrivate Browsing A feature in Internet Explorer 9 with which you can browse the Web without storing data about your browsing session; useful when using a public computer.

Internet Explorer 9 The Web browser software developed by Microsoft Corporation that is included with Windows 7.

Navigation bar On a Web page, a group of links used to navigate the site.

New Tab page A page that displays a list of sites that you have visited frequently.

Notification bar A bar at the bottom of an Internet Explorer screen that displays information about downloads, blocked pop-up windows, add-ons, and installing ActiveX controls.

Phishing A technique used to trick computer users into revealing personal or financial information through an e-mail message or a Web site.

Pop-up A small Web browser window that displays on top of the Web site you are viewing, and which are usually created by advertisers.

Pop-up Blocker A feature in Internet Explorer that enables you to block most pop-ups.

Portal A Web site that displays news, content, and links that are of interest to a specific audience.

Protected mode A feature in Internet Explorer that makes it more difficult for malicious software to be installed on your computer by preventing a downloaded program from making any direct changes to the system.

Protocol prefix The letters that represent a set of communication rules used by a computer to connect to another computer.

RSS An acronym for *Really Simple Syndication*, which is a syndication format popular for aggregating—gathering together—updates to blogs and news sites.

RSS feed Frequently updated content published by a Web site and delivered to a feed reader.

RSS viewer A program that displays RSS feeds to which you have subscribed.

Search provider A Web site that provides search capabilities on the Web.

Search term A word or phrase that describes the topic about which you want to find information.

Show Address bar Autocomplete button A button that displays a list of recently accessed Web locations, and which displays buttons for Web slices and search providers.

SmartScreen Filter A feature in Internet Explorer that helps detect phishing Web sites and Web sites that distribute malware.

Sponsored links Paid advertisements shown as links, typically for products and services related to your search term; sponsored links are the way that search sites like Bing, Google, and others earn revenue.

Suggested Sites In Internet Explorer 9, an optional online service that suggests other Web sites in which you might be interested based on the Web sites you visit most.

Surfing The process of navigating the Internet either for a particular item or for anything that is of interest, and quickly moving from one item to another.

Syndicated content Another name for an RSS feed.

Tab row The area across the upper portion of the Internet Explorer screen in which a tab for each open Web site displays.

Tabbed browsing A feature in Internet Explorer that enables you to open multiple Web sites in a single browser window.

Tear-off tab A feature of tabs which enables you to pin Web sites to the taskbar, and to open the tab site in a new window.

Temporary Internet files Copies of Web pages, images, and media that you have downloaded from the Web, which makes viewing faster the next time you visit a site that you have visited before.

Top level domain The ending letters of a URL such as *.com*, *.org*, and so on.

Uniform Resource Locator An address that uniquely identifies a location on the Internet.

URL The acronym for Uniform Resource Locator.

Web browser A software program with which you display Web pages and navigate the Internet.

Web feed Another name for an RSS feed.

Web log The term from which *blog* is derived; an online journal or column used to publish personal or company information in an informal manner.

Web Slice A specific *portion*—a slice—of a Web page to which you can subscribe, and which enables you to see when updated content, such as the current temperature, is available from a site.

Windows Defender A spyware scanning and removal tool included with Windows 7; it is also integrated into the free Microsoft Security Essentials program.

XML feed Another name for an RSS feed

Index

A

Accelerators feature, 41, 43–46
ActiveX, 32
ActiveX controls, 32
add-ons, 31–33, 36
adding RSS feeds to Favorites Center, 19
address bar, 3–4, 8
Atom feed format, 41
Autocomplete button, 4

B

Back button, 4
blocking pop-ups, 46–47
blogs (Web logs), 3
bookmark managers, 20. *See also* **Favorites Center**
browsers, Web, 3
browsing. *See also* **tabbed browsing**
  InPrivate Browsing, 23–24
  the Web, 3
browsing history, 20–23
buttons. *See* **specific buttons**

C

certificates, 49
Certification Authorities, 49
closing
  Internet Explorer 9, 13, 23
  tabs, 10, 12
  Web Slices, 43
Command bar, 22
cookies, 21, 24
copying Favorites list, 19
copyright laws, 29
cost of RSS feeds, 41
country codes, 5

D

data, personal, 49–50
default search providers, 35–37
deleting
  add-ons, 32
  browsing history, 21–23
  Favorites, 20
  Web Slices, 43
digital signatures, 32
domain names, 5–6
domains, top level, 5–6

E

e-mailing Web pages, 30
exporting Favorites list, 19
Extensible Markup Language (XML), 41
extensions, 6

F

Favorites bar
  hiding, 28
  naming sites on, 20
  using, 19–20
  Web Slices on, 41–43
Favorites Center, 15–16. *See also* **browsing history; Favorites list; RSS (Really Simple Syndication) feeds**
Favorites folders, 16–19
Favorites list
  copying, 19
  folder creation, 16–19
  importing/exporting, 19
  naming sites on, 18
  organizing, 16–19
  printing, 19
  saving Web sites to, 15, 18
feed formats, 41
feed readers, 38
feeds, 19, 37–41
file extensions, 6
file formats, 30
folders, Favorites list, 16–19
fonts, 26–28
footers, 25–26
form data, 24
formats
  feed, 41
  file, 30
Forward button, 4
Full Screen mode, 28

H

headers, 25–26
hiding the Favorites bar, 28
history, browsing, 20–23
History button, 9
history, Web page, 24
Home button, 4
home pages, 3
HyperText Transfer Protocol (HTTP), 5

I

images, 29–30
importing Favorites list, 19
InPrivate Browsing, 23–24
Internet, searching the, 35–37
Internet Explorer 9
  closing, 13, 23
  defined, 3
  starting, 3
  window elements, 4
Internet Explorer Gallery, 36

K

keyboard shortcuts, 13

L

laws, copyright, 29
links, sponsored, 35

M

malware, 47–48
mouse shortcuts, 13

N

naming
folders, 16
sites on Favorite list, 18
sites on Favorites bar, 20
navigating open tabs, 9–13
navigation bar, 11
New Tab button, 4
New Tab page, 6–7
Notification bars, 31, 46–47

O

opening
Favorite sites, 17
multiple browser windows (*See* tabbed browsing)
organization type file extensions, 6
organizing the Favorites list, 16–19

P

passwords, 21, 24
personal data protection, 49–50
phishing, 49
pictures, 29–30
Pop-up Blocker, 46–47
pop-ups, 46–47
portals, 24
Print preview, 24–25
printing
Favorites list, 19
pictures from Web pages, 30
previewing, 24–25
Web pages, 24–27
protected mode, 48
protection
from malware, 47–48
of personal data, 49–50
protocol prefix, 5

Q

quotation marks (""), 35

R

Recent Pages list, 6
Refresh button, 4
renaming sites on Favorites bar, 20
RSS (Really Simple Syndication) feeds, 19, 37–41
RSS viewer, 38

S

saving
Web page information, 28–30
Web sites in Favorites list, 15, 18
search providers, 35–37
search terms, 35
searching the Internet, 35–37
shortcuts
Favorites folder, 17–18
keyboard, 13
mouse, 13
navigating open tabs with, 9–13
taskbar, 13–15
Show Address bar, 4
Show Address bar Autocomplete, 6, 9
side-by-side tabs, 13–15
signatures, digital, 32
SmartScreen Filter, 49
sponsored links, 35
spyware, 48
starting Internet Explorer 9, 3
status bar, 4
Stop button, 4
subscribing to RSS feeds, 38–41
Suggested Sites feature, 46
surfing, 3
syndicated content, 37–41

T

tab lists, 9–13
tab row, 4
tabbed browsing
defined, 3
navigating between tabs, 9–13
side-by-side tabs, 13–15
taskbar shortcuts, 13–15
using, 3–9
tabs. *See also* **tabbed browsing**
closing, 12
navigating open, 9–13
side-by-side, 13–15
tear-off, 13–15
taskbars
navigating open tabs with, 9–13
shortcuts on, 13–15
tear-off tabs, 13–15
temporary Internet files, 21, 24
text size, 27–28
top level domains, 5–6

U

URLs (Uniform Resource Locators), 3

V

View favorites, feeds, and history button, 4
viewing
browsing history, 21–23
pop-up messages, 46–47
RSS feeds, 38–41
side-by-side tabs, 13–15
Web pages in Full Screen mode, 28
viruses, 47–48

W

Web, the, 6
Web browsers, 3
Web feeds, 37–41

Web logs (blogs), 3
Web page history, 24
Web pages
copyright laws and, 29
displaying in Full Screen mode, 28
e-mailing, 30
printing, 24–27
saving information from, 28–30
text size on, 27–28
Web sites
phishing on, 49
RSS feeds vs, 41
saving to Favorites list, 16, 18
Web Slices, 19, 41–43
window elements, Internet Explorer 9, 4
windows, opening multiple. *see* **tabbed browsing**
Windows Defender, 48
Windows Live Favorites, 20
World Wide Web (WWW), 6

X

XML (Extensible Markup Language), 41
XML feeds, 37–41

Z

zooming, 27–28